SNAPREVISE

SnapRevise Text Guide: An Inspector Calls by J. B. Priestley

Sarah Montgomery

Miralo Education Group Ltd owner of SnapRevise® trademark.
96 Drove Road, Weston-Super-Mare, BS23 3NW United Kingdom

www.snaprevise.co.uk

Title: An Inspector Calls by J. B. Priestley Text Guide
ISBN: 978-1-917424-90-5

Published by Miralo Education Group Ltd CN 15550989

Preface

Hello! My name is Sarah Montgomery and I am an actor, poet, and writer from Aberdeenshire, Scotland, but have been living and working in London for the past three years. From a young age, I could always be found with my nose in a book, so when it came to choosing what I might study at university, it was always going to be English Literature. So, in 2017, I moved to The University of Glasgow where I completed my MA (Hons) in English Literature and Theatre studies, graduating in 2021 with a 2.1. Subsequently, after almost two years of pandemic-induced television watching, I decided that I wanted to become an actor and was lucky enough to be accepted onto the MA Acting course at EAST 15 Acting School, where I graduated with Distinction in 2022.

Humanity has been coming together to tell, swap, and listen to stories since the Dark Ages, passing down tales of morality, adventure, and community for generations. Stories have always been a place of comfort for me; I have always wanted to travel to different places, meet exciting characters and follow their journeys. For me, this is why studying English is so important and so wonderful: it allows us to discover more about ourselves than we knew before and to go through often exciting, thrilling, or captivating stories to get there.

I studied *An Inspector Calls* whilst at school and the story has always stayed with me. I hope that, through this Text Guide, you'll learn to enjoy and analyse all of the intricacies of a story which, although nearly 80 years old, is just as relevant now as it was in 1945 and still has its place on the modern stage.

— Sarah Montgomery

Contents

Section 1

Nutshell Summary

"It is an evening in spring, 1912." In the industrial North-Midlands town of Brumley, an upper-middle class family are celebrating the engagement of their daughter to the heir of a rival factory **dynasty**. The Birling family is headed by Arthur, a self-made and **pragmatic** businessman. If Arthur is the patriarch or male head of the family, his wife Mrs Sibyl Birling is the matriarch; domineering and snobbish, Mrs Birling commands the household with all the authority of an Edwardian **socialite**. Their daughter Sheila is giddy, materialistic and childish, whilst their son Eric appears to be an **aloof** but handsome young man prone to drinking. Gerald Croft, Sheila's fiancé, is both charming and polite – everything that an eligible bachelor of the time should be. Their spring evening takes a sudden turn when Inspector Goole, a new edition to the local police force, arrives to inform the group of a tragedy: a woman, Eva Smith, has committed suicide by drinking bleach and has died in agony at the local infirmary. Whilst it is at first unclear how the family figure into the story, one by one, the inspector unveils the true reasons for the girl's demise.

First to be questioned is Mr Birling. He is shown a photograph of Eva Smith and remembers her as one of his former employees who was dismissed for her part in workers' strikes for higher pay. He refuses to take any accountability for this causing her death, but Inspector Goole confirms that this was the **catalyst** for Eva Smith's downfall.

Sheila becomes embroiled in the questioning too: it is revealed that Eva Smith was subsequently sacked from a shop assistant's job simply because Sheila was in a rotten mood after an embarrassing fitting and used her father's position to pressure the staff into firing her. Unlike her father, Sheila is obviously remorseful, and the audience sees her become more self-aware.

When Inspector Goole mentions that Eva Smith then changed her name to Daisy Renton, Gerald is startled and inadvertently reveals that he knew her too. Mrs Birling then enters to berate the Inspector for his **impertinence** and assert her social superiority over him, but to no avail. Continuing his investigation, Inspector Goole moves on to Gerald and we learn about his love affair with Eva Smith, now Daisy, during the previous summer, after rescuing her from a predatory man in a dubious part of town. It is implied that she may have been there as she resorted to prostitution to financially support herself. After finding her a place to stay and providing for her for a while, Gerald then breaks things off and leaves her **destitute** again. Having heard Gerald's story, Sheila hands him back her engagement ring and he leaves.

Dynasty: an inherited line of rulers, like an empire or powerful bloodline.

Pragmatic: sensible, realistic, practical.

Socialite: a prominent person in fashionable society.

Aloof: distant, unfriendly, emotionally detached.

Catalyst: a spark that causes or greatly accelerates an event.

Impertinence: rudeness, disrespect.

Destitute: completely poor and deprived of all money and resources.

Mrs Birling, still irritated by the Inspector, claims she does not recognise the girl from the photograph. It is then revealed she saw her only two weeks previously when Eva Smith appealed to a women's charity where Mrs Birling is an influential member. Although it is revealed that Eva Smith is now pregnant and destitute, Mrs Birling deemed her unworthy of help and having airs above her station, asserting her influence within the charity to convince them to refuse help. Mrs Birling accepts no responsibility for her actions, stating that if anyone is to blame, it is the father of her illegitimate child for not stepping up. Sheila, somehow guessing the truth, tries to stop her mother's comments but is unsuccessful. Mrs Birling believes the Inspector should do his duty by reprimanding the young man who got Eva Smith into this mess and demands that he leaves. The Inspector says he is waiting to do his "duty," and it becomes clear that Eric is the father of Eva Smith's child.

Eric retells a story of drinking in the same disreputable part of town as Gerald when he one day met Eva Smith. Due to his drunkenness, it seems Eric became forceful and insistent on going home with her. They have a short affair, resulting in her pregnancy. He tries to steal money from his father's company in order to support her, but this appals Eva and she refuses to take the money or see him again.

Decrying: denouncing, condemning, or strongly criticising.

Having questioned everyone, Inspector Goole comments on collective responsibility, **decrying** individual greed and warning of humanity's downfall should people like the Birlings not change their ways. The Inspector leaves the family shocked, broken, and arguing over whose fault it ultimately is that Eva Smith committed suicide. In the midst of this argument, Gerald returns with intriguing news: he has met a sergeant who knows nothing of Inspector Goole. As the group piece together their impressions of the Inspector and his questioning, they begin to suspect that he isn't a real policeman. Mr Birling contacts the police and confirms that there is no one of that name on the force. They then begin to wonder whether there has even been a suicide, noting that they may not have all seen the same photograph. Again, using his power and position, Mr Birling contacts the infirmary to check and finds that there has been no one brought in for committing suicide in weeks. Whilst Arthur, Sibyl and Gerald take this as good news and return to feeling **irreproachably** innocent, Sheila and Eric have been entirely changed by the evening and continue to feel a sense of culpability, even if their actions didn't lead to anyone's death. The phone rings once more and Mr Birling answers: the conversation is brief and short. He relays to the family that a young woman has been taken to the infirmary having died from drinking bleach and that a policeman will be along to question them.

Irreproachably: beyond criticism, unimpeachable, flawless.

Section 2

Background Information

J.B. Priestley

Life and politics

John Boynton Priestly was born in Bradford, West Yorkshire, in 1894. Raised in a working-class family, he was deeply shaped by the values and experiences of the northern labouring community. His mother died when he was very young, and he was raised largely by his father who was a schoolmaster. Priestley left school at 16 to work as a junior clerk at a wool office, but he continued his education through evening classes and voracious reading. After serving in World War I, where he was badly wounded, he attended Trinity Hall, Cambridge, studying literature and history. His war experiences profoundly influenced his political outlook, fostering a deep distrust of the ruling classes and a rejection of the complacency and arrogance of the British elite, cultivating his commitment to social justice.

He became a prolific author and public intellectual in the interwar years, eventually co-founding the Common Wealth Party during the Second World War, advocating for public ownership and democratic socialism. A lifelong socialist, Priestley championed equality, workers' rights, and public welfare. In the 1940s, he co-founded the Common Wealth Party, advocating for democratic socialism, and used his writing and radio broadcasting to campaign for post-war reform. These wartime broadcasts, 'Postscripts,' were immensely popular with the public but were eventually cancelled by the BBC, likely due to pressure from Churchill's government which viewed his opinions as too radical. He declined both a knighthood and a peerage, reflecting his lifelong suspicion of establishment honours. Priestley was also a founding member of the Campaign for Nuclear Disarmament (CND), showing his continued engagement with political and ethical issues until his death in 1984 at the age of 90.

Career as an author

Though publishing many novels and short stories throughout his life, Priestley's transition onto the stage in the 1930s was where he met the most praise and success, with plays like *Dangerous Corner* (1932) and *Time and the Conways* (1937). His works naturally reflected many of his political beliefs and lifelong commitment to the ideas of community and **class consciousness**. His writing and much of his work in the public eye was always politically and socially engaged, with Priestley seen as a spokesman for the everyday Englishman and an avid critic of class systems and stereotypes.

Class conscious: understanding one's own class position in society and acting in the best interests of the collective class.

He used his writing to challenge conservative ideologies and promote his vision of a fairer, more equitable society. Commenting on his work in 1962, Priestley stated: "I could not be entirely serious about anything, except the wellbeing of our society itself." Priestley remained a prominent figure in the literary and political zeitgeist well into the 1970s, being awarded the Order of Merit in 1977.

Literary context

Mystery and detective fiction

Priestley was deliberate in crafting a play that fused elements of realism with aspects of morality drama and detective fiction, creating a hybrid structure that challenges audience expectations. Set entirely in one room and unfolding in real time, the play adheres to the **Aristotelian unities** of place, time, and action – techniques typical of classical drama. However, the inclusion of the Inspector as a mysterious, almost supernatural figure who seems to know more than he logically could adds an uncanny quality that disrupts pure realism. His name, Goole, itself sounds like '**ghoul**,' suggesting that he may not be a conventional character at all. The play also incorporates the conventions of a **whodunnit**, keeping the audience engaged in uncovering the truth behind Eva Smith's death. However, instead of revealing one definitive culprit, Priestley reveals that all the Birlings are complicit in different ways, subverting the detective genre's usual aim of closure. Although you don't need to understand too much about the broader genre context, for your GCSE you should consider how this structural choice reinforces Priestley's theme: the collective guilt of society. No single character is solely responsible, but rather, each one's selfishness and lack of empathy contributes to the tragedy. This narrative approach keeps the audience intellectually and morally engaged, asking them to interrogate their own complicity in social issues.

Aristotelian unities: the three rules set out by Aristotle that plays should 1 be set in one location, 2 tell a story that takes place in less than one day, and 3 have all action contribute to the plot.

Ghoul: an evil ghost.

Whodunnit: a colloquial term for the genre of literature based on deducing who the murderer is (literally 'who done it!?').

The theatre

It is worth noting that the institution of theatre and the arts have always contained elements of elitism. In particular, the notion of being a theatregoer or a connoisseur of drama productions is typically a privilege only afforded to those of the upper and middle classes who are able to afford tickets even to this day. However, in the post-war environment of 1945 when this play debuted, going to the theatre was generally more affordable. Following the end of World War II, seats in the stalls or standing cost approximately 2 shillings and 6 pence, equating to £5.97 in 2025, whereas boxes or spaces higher up could be around 4 or 5 pounds, which would be the same as two days wages at the time or at least £220.62 nowadays. This means it is likely that audiences to the original London production of *An Inspector Calls* may have been from a wider variety of social backgrounds, and therefore representative of the class divide in the play itself.

Whilst Priestly had already received acclaim for his 1934 play *Eden End*, reviews after the opening of *An Inspector Calls* were mixed, to say the least: some found it "heavy" and too long, containing "no theatrical ethics" (Lionel Hale, *The Daily Mail*), whilst others found it a triumph of British theatre, with critic Stephen Hale calling it "the best **coup de théâtre** of the year."

Coup de théâtre: a highly successful theatre production (also a term used to describe a successful sudden plot twist, as seen in this play!).

Socio-historical context

Class commentary

The play is set in the fictitious North Midlands town of Brumley in spring 1912. This was a deliberate choice of Priestley's, so let's start by analysing the significance of the setting. The history of the North Midlands area has been dominated by its industrial importance since the Victorian era: many of the first factories, railways and other key enterprises began in the Midlands as part of the Industrial Revolution in the late 18th century to mid-19th century. Whilst Brumley is a fictional place, it represents the many towns and cities where the economy and lives of its people centred around industrial business. Using this locale, Priestley can draw upon his British audiences' knowledge of such towns and the people who lived there: both the prospering upper-class Mr Birlings and the struggling lower-class Eva Smiths. The characters in this town are **archetypes** audiences would be able to easily recognise, making their stories more relatable and compelling.

Archetypes: a typical example of blueprint.

Although written in the 1940s, Priestley chose to set the play in the spring of 1912. This choice impacts the audience's understanding of the play in two ways, historically and culturally. The economy of Britain in the early 1900s was controlled largely by private companies and individuals, like the Birlings, as the Liberal government adopted a **laissez-faire** policy, whereby the governing bodies do not intervene with the economic order. Because of this, businessmen like Mr Birling were able to control the workforce as they dictated the rate of growth. Many references to events of the time pop up throughout the play, notably with Mr Birling's mention of the Titanic and the impossibility of war as seen in quotes like "a few German officers talking nonsense and a few scaremongers here making a fuss about nothing."

Laissez-faire: a principle of not interfering; being 'hands off.' In capitalist businesses this is often associated with 'letting the market decide' and not getting involved via government regulations.

The time period between 1912 and the play's debut in 1945 saw much social and cultural change, including the sinking of the Titanic (1912), the Russian Revolution (1917), the women's suffrage movement (1928), and both World Wars – the last of which had only just ended and the consequences of which were still reverberating across the globe. Any audience watching the play has the advantage of this historical knowledge and can recognise just how wrong Mr Birling is about almost everything. This is a great examples of Priestley employing **dramatic irony** to add a layer of meaning to the play. It also distances his audience from his characters, making it easier for viewers to critique the characters' flaws or false beliefs, reinforcing the themes of subjectivity and uncertainty.

Dramatic irony: when the audience knows something the characters do not.

It is also important to acknowledge the cultural impact of Edwardian society at play within the text. Following the death of Queen Victoria in 1901 and the end of her 63 year reign, a newly emerging era under King Edward VII was still in its early days. As such, many of the sensibilities and ideologies of the Victorian era were still heavily accepted and adhered to, influencing aspects of daily life such as morality, attitudes towards women, and class division. Victorian morals were often centred around the religious teachings of the Church and Bible, creating the rigidity and **stoicism** that we now associate with people of the Victorian period. This influenced how many people led their day-to-day lives, looking to Christianity for moral guidance and fostering a conservative environment where values such as purity, honesty, sobriety, and charity were highly valuable, whereas outspokenness, individuality, and rebelliousness were frowned upon.

Stoicism: enduring pain or hardship without displaying emotion.

This, in turn, influenced gender roles within the time period and attitudes towards women. There was a clear binary between men and women: men were the bread-winners, heads of households, and the figures in society to be obeyed and in power, whilst women were seen as meek, sensitive, emotional, and suited only to being wives and mothers. Women were legally seen as the property of their fathers until they were married, when they became the property of their husbands. Where men were able to pursue any career they wanted to, women were not allowed to work in well-paid or high-ranking positions, often only being eligible for the domestic service (as servants) or in the 'sweated industries' in factories for long hours and very little pay. Furthermore, women of all classes were held to a much higher moral standard than men: the binaries of the **Madonna–Whore complex** were the categories by which women's moral behaviour were judged, with devastating repercussions for women who were seen to transgress from the ideals of purity and obedience; for example, any woman who had a child outside of marriage was then ostracised from society. The **claustrophobic** environment of Edwardian Britain is emulated within the play, with all of the action taking place within the Birlings' dining-room. The play's historical, political, and social context informs almost every element of the action, giving modern audiences the ability to compare their own context to that of the play.

Madonna–Whore complex: a psychological term for the tendency to categorise women as either saintly, motherly 'Madonnas' or depraved, promiscuous 'whores.'

Claustrophobic: oppressive, like a confined space.

Political ideology

One of the most vital lenses through which to understand *An Inspector Calls* is its underlying political ideology. Although the play is not an overt **manifesto**, Priestley's beliefs as a committed socialist permeate its themes, characters, and structure. Socialism, as opposed to capitalism, promotes collective ownership, equality, and the prioritisation of community welfare over personal profit. The play is a direct critique of the class hierarchy and the self-serving nature of capitalist individualism, particularly embodied in the character of Mr Birling who dismisses responsibility for anyone beyond his immediate family and business interests. In contrast, the Inspector can be interpreted as Priestley's spokesman, delivering the play's moral argument about shared responsibility and social conscience. This is especially prominent in the Inspector's final speech which explicitly warns that "we are members of one body." This metaphor underscores the interconnectedness Priestley believed society must recognise. The timing of the play's first production in 1945 – just after World War II and at the dawn/golden age of the **Welfare State** in Britain – is crucial context: audiences were reflecting on the costs of inequality and considering alternatives to the pre-war order. Thus, Priestley's message of collective accountability resonated powerfully then, and remains relevant today.

Manifesto: a political treaty that outlines key principles and policies.

Welfare State: the name given to a set of government policies post-WWII intended to create a social safety net.

Section 3

Scene-by-Scene Analysis

Stage directions

Mise-en-scene: the arrangement of scenery, props, and other elements in the staging of a play.

Portentous: self-important, pompous.

The text opens with a lengthy description of the **mise-en-scène** to accurately encapsulate the dining room of a traditional upper-middle-class suburban home. Within the first sentence, we learn that the dining room is in a house "belonging to a prosperous manufacturer," setting up potential expectations as to the type of characters we may be introduced to. Priestley details that the overall atmosphere of the set should be "heavily comfortable, but not cosy or homelike." This tells the reader that whilst the house may appear welcoming, there is no warmth within its walls, later explored through the family's interactions. The characters are introduced in detail within the stage directions: Mr Birling is indeed "**portentous**," his wife "cold," his daughter "rather excited," his son "not quite at ease," and Gerald "the easy well-bred young man-about-town." Through his descriptions of each character, Priestley allows audiences a glimpse into their personalities before any dialogue begins, allowing for an understanding of the environment he has created and perhaps encouraging a consideration of how the varying archetypes will interact throughout the play.

Act One

The play begins as the family have finished their dinner. Edna, the parlour maid, is clearing champagne glasses and dessert plates, replacing them with "a decanter of port, cigar box, and cigarettes." This distinction establishes the social standing of the family, revealing both their ability to afford these luxuries and their upholding of the traditional after-dinner split where men stayed in the dining room to drink and smoke while women went through to the drawing room. Mr Birling's first line to Edna is an assertion of power, praising her for giving them the port, and proceeding to recommend it to Gerald as the same port his father drinks. Priestley also specifies in the stage directions that, upon Edna's exit, Mr Birling "*clearly relaxes*" when no longer in the presence of his servants. This furthers the class divide present onstage as it suggests to the audience that, despite being her social superior, Mr Birling only truly relaxes around his own people, demonstrating his prejudice against the working classes.

The social etiquette of the Edwardian period is emphasised through the ensuing conversation where Mrs Birling **berates** her husband for discussing the food in front of their guest, Gerald. Mr Birling defends himself by saying that he was simply treating Gerald "like one of the family," further reinforcing the societal norms and class divide that deems Gerald worthy of being considered a family member where others like Edna are not. Priestley uses this opening scene to demonstrate the various dynamics at play within the family such as his depiction of the siblings bickering: Sheila remarks that Eric is "**squiffy**" and he tries to rebut this before being called an "ass." This is also the first indication to the audience that Eric has been drinking more than the other characters – an issue that rears its head throughout the play.

Berate: to chide or scold.

Squiffy: a slang word meaning drunk or tipsy.

In an attempt to defuse the argument now breaking out between Sheila and Eric, Mrs Birling reminds her husband that he should be making a speech, to which he obliges. It begins with a note that Gerald's parents, Sir George and Lady Croft, are abroad and unable to join their party, indicating Gerald's social superiority to the Birlings for the first time. Rather than a heartfelt speech to his daughter, Arthur Birling comes across as almost oblivious of his daughter's part in the union, exposing a potential lack of (or maybe just the inability to speak about) deep affection. He proceeds to discuss the now subdued rivalry between the two family businesses. Mrs Birling attempts to bring the speech more towards Sheila, scolding him for talking of business, with Sheila in agreement it was "all wrong." The speech ends with wishing the couple "the very best that life can bring" and the party toast to Gerald and Sheila, with Mrs Birling again evidencing more affection for Sheila through calling her "darling." She nudges Eric to join in the toast, and he remarks on Sheila's "nasty temper" as, Priestley **foreshadows** the impact of Sheila's attitudes and her thoughtlessness.

Foreshadows: when an author hints at events that will happen later in the text.

In contrast to Birling's almost clinical toast to their marriage, Sheila and Gerald share a tender moment where they "*look at each other*" and speak "*quietly*" amongst themselves, suggesting to the reader that their engagement is one founded on true affection. Gerald then proceeds to give Sheila her engagement ring, causing her great excitement: "Oh – it's wonderful! Look – Mummy – isn't it a beauty? Oh – darling –." The text mirrors her breathlessness and erratic nature, showing the excitement and pleasure she gains from this object. Priestley further demonstrates Sheila's materialistic nature when Mr Birling again begins to speak and she is oblivious: "*noticing that Sheila is still admiring her ring*". Establishing her as a naïve, **rapacious** girl, Priestley provides a basis from which his audiences and readers can see her evolution throughout the play, exploring the impact the Inspector and his words will have on her.

Rapacious: greedy, grasping for money.

Arthur Birling then delves into an indulgent speech where he decries the "silly talk" of the day, leaning instead on his instincts as a "hard-headed business man, who has to take risks and know what he's about," indicating his self-belief and confidence. He makes mention of the miner's strike which caused "wild talk" but reassures the rest of the party that they have "passed the worst of it," and that they're "in for a time of steadily increasing prosperity." Through this section, Priestley provides the audience and reader with the socio-political context of 1912, establishing the **tumultuous** landscape that the characters find themselves in. This is furthered through Birling's comments on the talk of an "inevitable" war, to which he responds "fiddlesticks!" He rebuffs the idea as ludicrous due to the innovations in fields such as technology and transport, leading him to comment on the "unsinkable, absolutely unsinkable" Titanic. His speech concludes by prophesying life in 1940, where he believes talk of "silly little war scares" and "Capital versus Labour agitations" will have been forgotten, with "peace and prosperity [...] everywhere." This heavy use of dramatic irony demonstrates to the audience the ignorant attitudes of upper-class society at the time, burying their heads in the sand and completely misjudging what the future holds. This limits the ability of readers and audience members to take Mr Birling seriously as their knowledge of the events of the early 20th century highlights his lack of awareness and understanding.

Tumultuous: turbulent, confusing, full of uncertainty.

Mrs Birling, Sheila, and Eric then move into the drawing room for coffee, leaving Mr Birling and Gerald. When offered a cigar, Gerald politely declines and opts instead for a cigarette: a symbol of wealth and refinement, Mr Birling's cigar represents his desire for opulence and status, whilst Gerald's cigarette could be suggestive of his transition from the older traditions he has grown up with to the young and modern world. Mr Birling's insecurity about social standing becomes even more apparent when he suggests to Gerald that Lady Croft feels he could have "done better" with a betrothal but reveals that he believes he might be in the running for a knighthood. This is **caveated** by a blasé remark about staying out of trouble: "so long as we behave ourselves, don't get into the police court or start a scandal – eh?". Through this, Priestley both foreshadows the imminent call from the Inspector and the **fickle** structure of Edwardian society, where any behaviour or incident deemed unsavoury could mean rejection and isolation.

Caveat: a warning about the conditions that must be adhered to.

Fickle: prone to changing on a whim; volatile, capricious.

Eric re-enters and pours himself another glass of port, again hinting at his drinking problem. He tells the men that he left his mother and sister discussing clothes "again," commenting that women "go potty" about such things, whilst Mr Birling corrects him that women think of their wardrobe as a "sign or token of their self-respect." Through this exchange, Priestley establishes the men's attitudes towards the women in their lives, clearly separating them into the distinct gender roles of the time, giving his audience an insight into Edwardian attitudes towards gender. Eric begins to say something in agreement, but thinks better of it, giving the audience the sense that he is hiding something.

Although he states he does not want to "lecture" Gerald and Eric again, Mr Birling launches into another indulgent speech, this time centring on the ideas of individualism. He declares that "a man has to make his own way" in the world, condemning the "cranks" who believe in collectivity, thinking of society "as if we were all mixed up together like bees in a hive – community and all that nonsense." The simile of bees in a hive demonstrates the closeness and interconnectivity of the species – a naturally occurring phenomenon that has connotations of great productivity and success, yet Mr Birling rejects it entirely as "nonsense." By introducing this conflict within the first act, Priestley sets this question up in the audience's mind, thereby making it a point of focus and allowing him to explore the argument effectively throughout the rest of the play.

Just as Mr Birling declares once again that "a man has to mind his own business and look after himself and his own," there is a "*sharp ring*" at the front door, interrupting the conversation. This is the first disruption to the established order of the Birlings' evening and lives. Edna enters and tells Mr Birling that an Inspector by the name of 'Goole' has called on them, with "important" business. After Gerald makes a snide comment that Eric may have been "up to something" (referencing the earlier conversation about avoiding scandal), Eric becomes agitated and "uneasy," saying he didn't find the joke funny. This behaviour again signals to the audience that he is hiding something, and that with the arrival of the Inspector, the truth may be revealed, creating a sense of anticipation and intrigue.

Much like the first introduction to the Birlings, Priestley provides a detailed description of the Inspector. Though the actor "*need not be a big man*," we are told that he "*creates at once an impression of massiveness, solidity and purposefulness*." Through this introduction, Priestley establishes Inspector Goole as a character who takes up space in the room, commanding and steady. The Inspector reveals he has just transferred to Brumley and, within seconds of their meeting, Mr Birling attempts to assert his station over him by drawing attention to his former positions as an **alderman** and Lord Mayor. The Inspector begins innocently by stating he would like "information", proceeding to tell the men that a young woman died in the local infirmary a few hours ago, having swallowed disinfectant earlier in the afternoon, detailing that it "burnt her inside out" and that she was in "great agony". He notes that it was suicide "of course", indicating to the audience that she wanted to take her own life, which was illegal in both 1912 and 1946; thus both the play's setting and its context amplify the sense of tragedy and gravity of such an action.

Alderman: a senior governing member on a local council, second-in-command to a mayor.

Mr Birling responds "rather impatiently," wanting to know how this involves him, indicating a reluctance and disinterest in her death, whilst Eric "involuntarily" exclaims "My God," evidencing the difference between the father and son. The audience and characters learn that her original name was Eva Smith, and Mr Birling states that whilst he does not remember *her*, he recognises her name but it "doesn't convey anything" to him. The Inspector tells him that she was once an employee of his, but Mr Birling shrugs it off as he has "several hundreds of young women [...] and they keep changing," alluding to the mass employment of working-class women in industrial factories in the early 20th century, but also underscoring that these are simply nameless, faceless workers to men like Mr Birling. The Inspector unveils a photograph he found of Eva Smith and suggests Mr Birling takes a look at it: when Eric and Gerald attempt to look for themselves, the Inspector steps between them and blocks their view, leaving them "*surprised and rather annoyed.*" Gerald, "*showing annoyance*," asks the Inspector why he shouldn't see the photograph, with Eric arguing the same. The Inspector cryptically states that there might be a reason and that it is the way he likes to work, going around and talking to one person at a time to avoid a "muddle," establishing his power within the scene and confirming that from now on, the family must follow his lead.

Revealing that he now remembers Eva Smith, Birling states that he "discharged" her from her role, using a euphemism to distance himself from the harsh economic consequences of his actions for a working-class woman. He explains that she worked for him in the autumn of 1910, and Gerald asks whether Mr Birling would rather he left, but Birling says he doesn't mind, introducing the Inspector to his future son-in-law: "Perhaps I ought to explain first that this is Mr Gerald Croft – the son of Sir George Croft – you know, Crofts Limited." The repetition and emphasis on Gerald's surname demonstrates the importance of his family (if only in Mr Birling's mind), as if this should in some way impress the Inspector. Upon learning of Gerald and Sheila's engagement, the Inspector states "*gravely*" that he'd prefer Gerald to stay, foreshadowing that he too will undergo the Inspector's interrogation later.

Mr Birling once more attempts to distance himself from the investigation, claiming that something that happened nearly two years ago has "nothing whatever to do with the wretched girl's suicide." The Inspector, however, explains that there was a "chain of events" leading to her death. Through this metaphor, Priestley demonstrates how lives can be interlinked and the effect of one action upon the next. Still, Mr Birling rejects this, stating that he "can't accept any responsibility" and that "if we were all responsible for everything that happened to everybody we'd had anything to do with, it would be very awkward." This again poses the question of collective responsibility in the minds of the audience, compelling us to ask who is responsible and to what extent.

The audience is now given a description of Eva Smith for the first time by Mr Birling, saying she was "a lively good-looking girl [...] a good worker too" who was headed for a promotion. A dispute then began about a pay increase, which Mr Birling "of course" refused. When asked why, Mr Birling gets irritated and begins to critique the Inspector's tone and questions, going on to explain that his "duty" is to keep labour costs down. Despite allowing everyone else to return after the strike, several of those who had spearheaded the pay dispute were told to "clear out", including Eva Smith who had "far too much to say."

Mr Birling exposes his class prejudices once more as he claims that "if you don't come down sharply on some of these people, they'd soon be asking for the earth." Eric continues to show his support for the workers, asking why they shouldn't try for higher wages as "we try for the highest possible prices," leading his father to claim it is "about time you learn to face a few responsibilities."

Just as Mr Birling begins to ask what happened to Eva Smith after she was dismissed from the factory, Sheila re-enters "gaily," a complete tonal shift from the intensity of the investigation. When the Inspector tries to get Sheila to stay after her father tells her to leave, Birling again becomes agitated, saying he finds the questioning "**officious**." Priestley demonstrates here that Mr Birling is rattled by this challenge to his own authority. The Inspector explains to Sheila why he is there and the details of Eva Smith's death shock her, causing her to be "*distressed*." This show of sympathy from Sheila, similar to that of her brother, demonstrates the link between the two in their empathy for others, further distancing them from their parents. Gerald tries to remind the Inspector that the important part of his investigation is to find out what happened to Eva Smith after she was fired, which he tells him none of them know anything about, leading the Inspector to ask "[*slowly*] Are you sure you don't know?" Through this comment, the audience learns at the same time as the characters that there is a probability they are all involved in some way with Eva Smith's death, creating tension in an already heightened environment, leaving the characters "*bewildered*." This leads Mr Birling to attempt to **renege** his previous critiques of the Inspector, apologising as "this makes a difference."

Officious: asserting authority in a domineering, self-important way.

Renege: to go back on or withdraw an offer or agreement.

The Inspector reveals that, following her dismissal, Eva Smith was left almost destitute "with no relatives [...] lonely, half starved [and] desperate," eliciting more sympathy from Sheila who reminds her father that "these girls aren't cheap labour." Eva Smith eventually had a "wonderful stroke of luck" and was employed at Milward's clothes shop, which Sheila says she frequents, only to be dismissed again a few months later after a customer complained about her. Sheila becomes "*agitated*" and asks to see the photograph whereupon she "*recognises, gives a half-stifled sob, and runs out*," causing Mr Birling to once again accuse the Inspector of making a "nasty mess" of their evening. Eric expresses a desire to leave, but The Inspector makes a grave statement observing that he ought to stay, to which Gerald professes that they are "respectable citizens and not criminals." The Inspector remarks upon the reality that "there isn't as much difference as you think," **elucidating** the question of appearance versus reality and the ambiguities between good and evil.

Elucidate: to shine light on.

Upon Sheila's return, she reveals how she put pressure on the shop owners to fire Eva Smith during a visit, simply because she was jealous that she looked better in a dress than her: "she was the right type for it, just as I was the wrong type [...] and I was absolutely furious." Sheila condemns her own materialistic nature and her behaviour, declaring instant regret, only to have the Inspector remind her that it is "too late" for such remorse. Unlike her father, Sheila acknowledges her part in Eva's downfall, demonstrating a culpability not yet witnessed by the audience and thereby a signal of hope that there can be some important moral change within the story.

The Inspector "*sternly*" stresses the severity of the consequences for Eva Smith, stating he will not leave until he knows "all that happened," outlining again the motif of truth within the play. When he remarks that she had subsequently changed her name to Daisy Renton, Gerald is startled and pours himself a drink, exposing his involvement in her demise. The Inspector leaves the room to find Mr Birling and Sheila wastes no time in questioning Gerald who in her words "gave [himself] away." He tries to shake her off, **placating** her with the affirmation of "darling" but Sheila powers ahead: she bombards him with questions about how and when he knew the girl but is met with silence. Gerald asks her not to tell the Inspector and Sheila calls him a "fool," as she understands the gravity of the situation: "*he knows* [...] And I hate to think how much he knows that we don't yet. You'll see." This intense exchange and premonition on Sheila's part mirrors the audience's journey alongside the characters, discovering the truth as the action unfolds. The intensity Priestley creates through this culminates in the Inspector's return and simple question of "well?" as he looks "*steadily*" at Gerald, waiting to be told the next part of Eva Smith's tragic story.

Placate: to appease, calm, or soothe negative emotions.

Act Two

Act Two picks up from the established tension at the end of the first act, with the Inspector re-entering to begin his investigation. Gerald asks that Sheila be excused from the rest of the questioning, implying that her mental state is not strong enough to hear any more. Sheila sums this up succinctly by telling the Inspector "he means that I'm getting hysterical now." Whilst she acknowledges this may indeed be the case, it also draws attention to stereotypes of feminine fragility and sensibility recognised within Edwardian society. She states, however, that she is going to stay, much to Gerald's **chagrin**, as he suggests she wants to "see somebody else put through it." They quarrel as Sheila says that he must now see her as a "selfish, vindictive creature" but the Inspector interrupts to clarify why he believes Sheila wishes to remain: "She feels responsible. And if she leaves us now, and doesn't hear any more, then she'll feel she's entirely to blame." He remarks that "if there's nothing else, we'll have to share our guilt," returning again to the notion of community.

Chagrin: annoyance or frustration at having failed.

The atmosphere shifts once more as Mrs Birling re-enters "*briskly and self-confidently*," something Sheila feels "*at once*." Her tone when addressing the Inspector is both condescending and defensive trying to intimidate the Inspector by asserting her social status. Sheila attempts to steer her mother in a different way, stating that she is "beginning all wrong" and that she will "say or do something that you'll be sorry for afterwards." Mrs Birling notes that Inspector Goole has made "a great impression on the child" to which he replies that they "often do on the young ones. They're more impressionable." Priestley openly addresses the rigidity and reluctance of older generations to accept change or new ways of thinking, something that may indeed lead to their downfall as the play continues.

This conflict between Sheila and her mother continues, with Sheila desperately trying to correct her mother's attitude of trying to "build up a kind of wall" between them and Eva Smith. The wall symbolises the many divides between the classes: opportunity, wealth, power, and autonomy. It allows the audience to see the physical barriers that the working classes are denied in the current system, hinting that a society founded on an ideology of equality would allow everyone the same opportunities and freedoms. Mrs Birling, choosing to ignore Sheila's pleas, continues in her attempt to intimidate the Inspector by asserting her social status, stating his attitude is "impertinent" and attempting to re-establish the power dynamics she associates with her station. Brushing her off, the Inspector attempts to find out where Mr Birling and Eric are, and is told that Eric is in an "excitable silly mood" due to his drinking. Mrs Birling states he is "only a boy," infantilising him as she does with Sheila. When she tells the Inspector that he doesn't drink heavily, Sheila and Gerald reveal to her that Eric does "drink pretty hard" and has done so for "the last two years," a shocking revelation to Mrs Birling.

In showing Mrs Birling's lack of understanding with Eric's drinking, Priestley further cements the lack of closeness between the Birling parents and their children, allowing him to use them as opposing sides within the presentation of his themes.

Mr Birling re-enters and argues with the Inspector about Eric staying up, as it is stated that Eric must "wait his turn." Birling accuses him of mishandling the inquiry and states he doesn't want to give him "much more rope," whereupon Sheila laughs "*rather wildy*" and makes a grave comment: "No, he's giving us rope – so that we'll hang ourselves." Her understanding of what is afoot is evident, the violent image of the "rope" and allusion to execution conveying the severity of their situation, contrasting with the ignorance of her parents.

Inspector Goole pulls the conversation back towards Eva Smith, and details once again how she became Daisy Renton, blatantly telling Gerald he gave himself away "at once" upon hearing her name. Gerald confesses reluctantly that he met her at the Palace Bar, an establishment frequented by "women of the town," euphemistically referencing prostitutes. He details how he rescued her from a "half-drunk and goggle-eyed" alderman known to the family, something which shocks Mr and Mrs Birling. Sheila claims that Alderman Meggarty's repudiation is well known, stating a girl she knows "only escaped with a torn blouse." This demonstrates that the assumed moral superiority of the upper classes is simply a façade, exemplifying how many can ignore the truth of a person just because of their title. Priestley also uses this exchange to again comment upon **misogynistic** attitudes towards women and the violence they face within everyday life.

Misogyny: disrespect or hatred towards women.

Removing her from the Palace Bar (and therefore from a place of moral degradation) Gerald takes 'Daisy' to the County Hotel and buys her a drink: through their conversation, he learns about her past but also that she is "desperately hard up" and almost destitute. Seeing how she is vulnerable and mistreated, Gerald rescues her, giving her money, and housing her temporarily in a friend's apartment. An affair ultimately begins, even though he states he "didn't ask for anything in return," adoring his presence as the hero in her life – the "fairy prince" as Sheila puts it. Just before he has to go away for business, Gerald ends their relationship, stating Daisy was "very **gallant**" about the whole thing. Gerald exposes the selfishness of his actions, the ease with which he seems to discard her speaking to contemporary attitudes towards women, something which echoes throughout the play. With his part in the questioning done, Gerald asks to leave and have some time alone as he is "upset" by this "business." Sheila, who is understandably hurt but also appreciative of Gerald's honesty, returns her engagement ring, symbolising the end of their relationship and her increasing levels of maturity, declaring that "You and I aren't the same people who sat down to dinner here."

Gallant: brave, heroic.

Upon Gerald's departure, Mrs Birling attempts to conclude proceedings but Inspector Goole insists on showing her the photograph. She states that she does not recognise the girl and is accused of "not telling [...] the truth," a comment which is met with outrage from both Mr and Mrs Birling. They demand an apology, but the Inspector retorts that he is only doing his "duty," thereby highlighting the inherent search for the truth within the play and within the Inspector's character as his driving motivation. Sheila establishes herself firmly on-side with the Inspector, saying that their rudeness, dishonesty and attempt at intimidating him by "putting on airs" is "making it worse," alluding to the concealment of the truth. The sound of a door slamming is heard and Mr Birling leaves to find out if it was Eric.

The Inspector now begins to question Mrs Birling, confirming that she is a "prominent" member of Brumley Women's Charity Organisation, helping women "in distress" appeal for aid and doing "useful work" in "deserving cases," as Mrs Birling puts it. Mr Birling re-enters and states it must have been Eric in "one of his excitable **queer** moods" but that it is of little consequence as he isn't needed, only to be told by the Inspector that, if he isn't back soon, they will need to find him. It is then revealed that Mrs Birling saw Eva Smith "only two weeks ago," causing shock amongst her family which Priestley demonstrates through short sentences, one of the first instances in the play. This creates a shift in pacing, emphasising the importance of the revelation. Mrs Birling recounts that Eva Smith presented herself as "Mrs Birling" and behaved with "gross impertinence," leading her to be "prejudiced" against her case. She catches her out in a number of lies about her identity as Mrs Birling, and concludes that she wasn't "satisfied" with her appeal for help and considers she "did [her] duty" in using her influence to sway the rest of the committee against giving her aid.

Queer: in this era meaning strange or out-of-character, as opposed to the contemporary meaning in terms of sexual identity.

Mrs Birling's coldness and **apathy** is demonstrated in her **stalwart** belief she did "nothing wrong." However, the Inspector challenges that she will "spend the rest of [her] life regretting it," finally dropping the metaphorical bomb that Eva Smith was pregnant. This horrifies Sheila who calls her mother "cruel and vile" and even Mr Birling (thinking as ever of his reputation) says that if the story came out it wouldn't "do [them] much good." Mrs Birling lashes out, straying from her collected appearance as an untouchable socialite to berate her family for their part in the girl's suicide, claiming that she was "justified" in her actions and that she told Eva Smith to look for the child's father as it was his "responsibility."

Apathy: a lack of emotion or empathy.

Stalwart: staunch, unmoving.

She reiterates that Eva Smith was "giving herself ridiculous airs" which were "simply absurd for a girl in her position," only to be countered by the Inspector who provides another brutally incisive, "stern" retort: "Her position now is that she lies with a burnt-out inside on a slab." The infrequent reminders of the visceral and grotesque nature of Eva Smith's death echoes the indifference of the characters questioned, with Priestley reminding the audience of the very real consequences their actions have caused and the terrible pain this young woman experienced, thereby commenting on the short-lived sympathy of the upper classes for those living in poverty.

When questioned about this mysterious father, Mrs Birling recounts that he was apparently "silly and wild" and that Eva Smith wouldn't accept money he had tried to give her as she thought it was stolen. When asked who is to blame for the girl's death, Mrs Birling states it is both Eva Smith's own fault but also the father of her child and that he should be "made an example of," naming him the "chief culprit" if her story of the stolen money was true. Sheila, "*with sudden alarm*," begs her mother to stop but is dismissed, with Mrs Birling continuing to tell the Inspector it is his "duty" to reprimand and publicly shame the young man. She concludes their interaction is now finished and begins to bid him goodnight; however, the Inspector dramatically tells her he is indeed "waiting" to do his "duty."

The act climaxes with the Mr and Mrs Birling's "*thunderstruck*" realisation that Eric is the father of Eva Smith's child. Priestley's descriptions communicate the extent of their fear and shock upon discovering the truth, playing upon the weight a scandal such as this would carry within the play's historical context. The "scandal" so feared by Mr Birling has appeared in the shape of his own son, allowing the audience to see the extent to which a revelation like this would shake an upper class family of the time. Mr and Mrs Birling's ignorance and distance from the reality of their children's lives and actions is made clear, further highlighting the dynamic of upper class Edwardian families. Sheila continues chastising her mother, having "begged and begged" her to stop her tirade against the man it is obvious is actually Eric, but is silenced by the Inspector as he simply "holds up a hand" – he is in complete control of the situation. "*We hear the front door*" just before the curtain falls, and the audience sees Eric's "*distressed*" face as he is confronted by his family's "*inquiring stares*." The audience is once again thrown into chaos in anticipation of the next act's revelations.

Act Three

The final act begins at this same moment of tension: the revelation Eric was the father of Eva Smith's baby. Unlike the others, he doesn't attempt to hide his involvement and simply asks "You know, don't you?" Mrs Birling is "distressed" over what she has been saying, with Sheila telling Eric that their mother thought the man involved "shouldn't escape." They squabble when Eric finds out his drinking habits have been exposed, calling Sheila a "sneak." She defends her decision to be honest, further reminding the audience of the contrast between the members of the family, exemplified when Mr Birling suggests that Sheila should have a "sense of loyalty" to them. The Inspector "*smoothly*" cuts in, again steering the conversation back to his objective.

Eric, having poured himself another drink, recounts how he met Eva Smith at the Palace Bar when he was already "a bit squiffy" and bought her a few drinks. It is alluded that she may have been driven to work as a prostitute, with the mention another woman had wanted her to go to the bar. The Palace Bar once again acts as a place of contradiction, seemingly **opulent** and wealthy on the surface whilst also being the site for seedy, illicit activity and drunkenness so despised by Edwardian morality. Eric notes that he "insisted" in going home with her, that he was in "that state when a chap easily turns nasty" and that she reluctantly lets him in, implying a non-consensual sexual encounter, though the play avoids explicit language. Eric's remorse is evident as he describes being unable to remember the "hellish" details, exclaiming "my God!" As Mrs Birling's distress becomes more evident, Mr Birling asks Sheila to escort her out, which she reluctantly agrees to do as she wants to hear the rest of his story.

Opulent: ostentatious, luxurious.

Eric goes on to tell them he happened to see Eva Smith again at the Palace Bar and this time, when they go home together, they talk more. They begin their affair but Eric admits he "wasn't in love with her or anything" and calls her a "good sport," evidencing the exploitation of working class women by men of privilege as he uses her only for his own drunken amusement. He reveals she told him she was pregnant soon afterwards and that he was "in a hell of a state about it." When asked by the Inspector if she wanted to get married, Eric replies that she didn't want to because she knew he didn't love her, and that she infantilised him: "In a way, she treated me – as if I were a kid." This demonstrates Eric's lack of understanding and maturity, contrasting with Eva Smith's experience and the knowledge she gained as a result of her hardships, thereby highlighting the divide between upper and working class lives.

It is then revealed that Eric stole money from his father's business, just as Mrs Birling bursts back in with Sheila close behind. Mr Birling "*angrily*" berates Eric, showing his lack of compassion by calling him a "damned fool" and questions why he didn't just come to his father about it all. Eric exposes the distance and coldness in their relationship, saying Mr Birling is "not the kind of father a chap could go to when he's in trouble," thereby evoking sympathy from the audience as it reaffirms the absence of a traditional, supportive father–son relationship. Just before Mr Birling erupts over this comment, Inspector Goole states he is running out of time and that they can "divide the responsibility" after he has left. He confirms with Eric that Eva Smith refused any more money once she found out it was stolen, highlighting her strong moral character, and that she told Eric she didn't want to see him again. Sheila, the beacon of truth once more, tells Eric that Mrs Birling spoke to her, leading to a bombardment of questions from him. Priestley indicates an escalation of tension here through Eric's repeated questions, paradoxical to the Inspector's "*calm authority*" when he tells him about Mrs Birling's rejection of her plea for help. Eric, "*nearly at breaking point*," accuses his mother of "killing" her, repeating this as he becomes more frenzied, damning her for the murder of her own grandchild. The family descends into chaos, a far cry from the refined dinner party the audience first saw them as, exposing the **façade** of upper-class etiquette.

Façade: a false or deceptive outward appearance.

Just as we sense a fight may break out, the Inspector "*masterfully*" commands them to stop and listen to him. He concludes that each member of the family helped to kill Eva Smith and calls on them to "remember that." He summarises their involvement one by one, using emotive language to drive home the catastrophic nature of their behaviour. Mr Birling attempts to bribe the Inspector with "thousands," showing he has not learned anything from this encounter and that he still subscribes to a capitalist ideology that money can fix anything. The Inspector "**sardonically**" surveys the family, noting that he doesn't think any of them will forget what they did and that at least they "cannot do her any more harm," cannot even apologise to her. He then begins the play's most famous extract, a speech rallying the Birlings to remember "we don't live alone. We are members of one body. We are responsible for each other," contrasting directly with and exposing the idiocy of Mr Birling's earlier speech. The audience is reminded of the interconnectedness of society and the importance of social responsibility over class, status or wealth.

Sardonically: sarcastically, mockingly, with a grim cynicism.

We are further reminded that this was only one girl's story but that "there are millions and millions and millions of Eva Smiths and John Smiths still left with us, with their lives, their hopes and fears, their sufferings," reasserting the often catastrophic suffering of ordinary people at the hands of the ignorant and privileged few. Priestley uses the Inspector to advocate for his political message of equality and social connectivity, leaving the Birlings with a bleak warning: "the time will soon come when, if men will not learn that lesson, then they will be taught it in fire and blood and anguish." This violent image of a hellish lesson foreshadows the horrors of the First World War – by playing upon an event that may very well have affected every member of his audience in some way, Priestley grounds his play further in their own reality and uses this tangible consequence of human cruelty to drive home his political and moral message. Bidding the family a swift and blunt "good night," Inspector Goole leaves and the "*subdued*" family is now faced with the aftermath of this life-changing interaction.

After the Inspector leaves, Priestley returns to explore the divide between the older and younger generation within the family. Mr Birling wastes no time in returning to his anger with Eric, placing the blame directly at his feet: "You're the one I blame for this." He shows his concern about scandal, reputation, and the potential loss of his knighthood. Eric "*hysterically*" retorts that it doesn't matter, showing his loss of interest in material objects. Mrs Birling joins her husband and declares she is "absolutely ashamed" of her son, with Eric echoing her words to express his disapproval of his parents. Sheila, too, uses the same word, emphasising the place that shame holds within the consequences of their actions. She berates her family for pretending that "nothing much has happened" as they "don't seem to have learnt anything". They argue over what matters and what doesn't, with Mrs Birling ironically referring to Sheila as "childish" – the audience knows that Sheila is the most aware and mature of the family, proven even more plainly when she expresses a feeling that Inspector Goole "never seemed like an ordinary police inspector." Mr Birling latches onto this, critiquing once more his rudeness and way of speaking, calling him "prejudiced from the start [...] a Socialist or some sort of crank." Again, Priestley uses irony to hint at the hypocrisy of the upper classes. Mrs Birling then hushes her "children" so that Mr Birling can "decide what [they] ought to do," drawing attention to the gender stereotypes of the day.

The doorbell rings again and they all "*look at each other in alarm*," now on-edge at the thought they will be confronted again. Gerald appears, asking when the Inspector left them and how he was behaving, told by Sheila he was "frightening." He goes on to reveal that the Inspector was not a police officer, having met and confirmed with a sergeant he knows that "there wasn't any Inspector Goole or anybody like him on the force here." Mr Birling decides to ring up the Chief Constable, using his influence to get the information he wants. He describes the Inspector, listens, and then bids the Chief Constable good night. He hangs up the phone and reveals that "there's no Inspector Goole on the police" and that "as Gerald says – we've been had."

Mr Birling is overjoyed, stating this "makes a difference" but Sheila "[*bittlery*]" notes that it doesn't make them all "nice people." As Eric grows restless, he and Sheila agree that they "take too much" interest in what happened, demonstrating the introspective nature of the younger generation and Priestley's hope for them. Mrs Birling attempts to restore some of the Edwardian sensibilities of upper class society by telling Sheila to "behave sensibly" but Eric reminds her that, although they are pretending that "nothing's really happened at all" – a girl is still dead. He reminds them that what they did still happened, that it's "the same rotten story," thereby emphasising the degradation of their morality.

Gerald proposes that there is "no more real evidence" of the girl's death than there was that the Inspector was a police officer. He examines the Inspector's methods of "very artfully" using the smallest hints of information to get the family to confess their involvement, and "*triumphantly*" poses the question that it may not have all been the same girl. As they cannot confirm that they all saw the same photograph, or that one girl changed her name to Daisy Renton, they wonder whether the Inspector was "lying all the time" – excuses and justifications which Mr Birling laps up "*eagerly*." When Gerald surmises that elements of the investigation may have all been "nonsense," Priestley once again uses repetition to expose the idiocy of his words through Eric's response: "I don't see much nonsense about it when a girl goes and kills herself." Birling "*triumphantly*" examines the night's circumstances and concludes that, whoever the Inspector was, he decided to play a joke on them: "No police enquiry, No one girl that all this happens to. No scandal."

In order to find out decisively, Gerald gets the idea to ring up the infirmary. Priestley again exposes the misuse of power by the upper classes as, just by mentioning his family name and the company, Gerald is able to extract any information or value from other people as he sees fit. When he puts down the telephone, he tells the family that the infirmary hasn't had a suicide "in months" and that "no girl has died there today." Mr and Mrs Birling are both elated and begin to pour out some drinks. Sheila, however, doesn't lose sight of the fact that "everything [they] said had happened really had happened," suggesting they cannot act as if they are completely innocent. Mr Birling behaves "*jovially*", making fun of the Inspector while Sheila makes a move to leave, saying that the way he talks "frightens" her.

Whilst Arthur, Sibyl and Gerald return to feeling irreproachable and innocent, Sheila and Eric have been entirely changed by the evening and continue to feel a sense of culpability, even if their actions didn't lead to anyone's death, thereby demonstrating the younger generation's ability to change. Sheila seriously tells her father that the evening and Inspector were "anything but a joke," stating that even though they all "began to learn something" her parents have now "stopped." She reiterates the warning of learning their lesson through "fire and blood and anguish," showing she has taken it to heart, as has Eric who agrees it "frightens" him too. Gerald agrees with Mr Birling that "everything's all right now" and brazenly attempts to give Sheila the engagement ring back.

As Mr Birling describes the situation as a "joke" and openly ridicules his daughter, the phone rings once more. The conversation is brief, with Mr Birling listening intently. The caller hangs up and Mr Birling looks at the others in a "*panic-stricken fashion*." He relays to the family that a young woman has been taken to the infirmary having died from drinking bleach and that a policeman will be along to question them. They all stand "*guiltily and dumbfounded*" as the curtain falls, with Priestley creating a successfully tense and shocking coup de théâtre.

This twist blurs the line between reality and illusion: was the Inspector a supernatural figure, a moral conscience, or merely a dramatic device? The uncertainty surrounding his identity, and the repetition of the girl's death, suggests a cyclical moral reckoning. This also leaves us with plenty of other questions: would people change their attitudes and behaviours if confronted with the consequences, or are some people incapable of change and empathy? Does it matter if Eva Smith is one person connected to each family member, or multiple people that each of them have harmed? To what extent can any one person be considered culpable for the suffering of another? Priestley denies his audience closure, compelling them to grapple with the implications of personal and collective responsibility. The ambiguity reinforces the play's central message: social change requires constant vigilance. By leaving the future unresolved, Priestley challenges viewers not to consider their own ethical choices in a society that often repeats its failures.

Section 4

Character Analysis

Mr Birling

Arthur Birling is a self-aggrandising figure and the central point of the play from which we can extrapolate all key themes and messages. As the character with the most to say in the opening of the play, Mr Birling is our first and most stringent exposure to the ideologies of the world of this text, so we are encouraged to compare contrasting beliefs against what *he* has proclaimed.

He is a "hard-headed business-man" through and through; his goals in his life seem to be based entirely around money and power. His disdain for the workers' strike within his own factory demonstrates his lack of empathy for those desiring better wages, stating it is his "duty to keep labour costs down." He is a self-described "sound useful party man," indicating his support for the Tory Party, and talks excitedly about the potential of a knighthood. Described by Priestley from the outset as "portentous," connoting a pompousness and desire to impress, Birling is implied to be over-asserting himself in every situation, trying desperately to make himself equal to Gerald, whom he sees as superior in status. This behaviour is repeated through his interactions with the Inspector and suggests a deep-rooted insecurity within Birling: every decision he makes and action he takes is in order to showcase to others his power or status – to fit in with those he sees as the upper echelons of society and, in turn, who he wants to be perceived as. When talking to the Inspector, Mr Birling is often shown to be fighting to maintain authority, lashing out at the Inspector when he is challenged or when he feels his power is threatened, demonstrating his insecurity around social standing and a prejudice against the lower classes.

Mr Birling is also quick to establish his authority as the patriarch of the family, demanding respect from all those around him. Although Mr Birling is from a comparatively lower background than his wife, Priestley demonstrates how even Sibyl Birling invokes her husband's authority on numerous occasions to the Inspector in off-hand remarks like "you know of course that my husband was Lord Mayor only two years ago." It is also clear, however, that Mr Birling needs to be corrected by his wife on matters of social etiquette; for example, talking about business during a dinner party is apparently a big no-no! Theirs does not appear to be a marriage of much warmth, affection, or candour; there is no display of intimacy between husband and wife throughout the entire play, thereby reinforcing Edwardian conventions of propriety and stoicism, though this does not endear us to either character as they seem as devoid for genuine love for each other as they are devoid of empathy for anyone else.

With his children, it is clear that Mr Birling sees them both still as youngsters in need of guidance. Whilst this manifests in gentle yet firm corrections for Sheila, he reprimands Eric with much more severity, telling him to "just be quiet" and calling him a "damned fool." Sheila is his little girl, but he expects more of Eric simply because he is the son and heir of the family, playing with gendered stereotypes and the consigned gender roles of both the Edwardian and post-war era. The audience sees how Eric bears the brunt of his father's anger through the evening, talking to him "*savagely*", "*angrily*" and "*stormily*" as indicated by the stage directions – this diction does not exactly conjure ideas of fatherly affection!

Priestley uses Mr Birling's **trajectory** as an **allegory** for capitalism and greed. Throughout the play, Arthur is shown again and again to be focused on his business, his social standing and his wealth. These are his priorities and his family almost seem to be an after-thought. For instance, any fatherly affection in his speech for Sheila's engagement is overshadowed by the multiple mentions that, through Gerald, they are now closer to the status of landed gentry, with all the money and influence that affords. Whilst it is evident that Mr Birling is self-made and wasn't always in this privileged position, Priestly demonstrates through his greed and obsessions that he has fallen victim to the charms of capitalism. Mr Birling commands the dining room as he might command a board meeting at his factory, indulging in lengthy speeches and professing to the rest of the group as if his word is gospel. Indeed, when questioned by the Inspector about his dismissal of Eva Smith, he maintains an indifference and distance to her demise by claiming his actions couldn't have contributed to her life as he is utterly self-involved. Despite being obviously shaken by the Inspector's investigation, it is clear that this is not due to being forced to reflect on his own morality or behaviour, but out of fear of how it will ultimately damage his reputation. Once convinced that the Inspector and the suicide are a hoax, he quickly begins to act as if nothing has happened and "*triumphantly*" rejects the idea that things have changed, stating: "the whole thing's different now." He acts as if the whole evening has been a "joke", returning to his original carefree and authoritative demeanour, thereby representing the power of capitalism, the complacency of the privileged, and the sinister power of the status quo within Priestley's society at the time, and indeed our own contemporary one.

Trajectory: the movement or journey a character undergoes throughout a text.

Allegory: a story with a hidden moral or political meaning.

Mrs Birling

Immovable in her morals and beliefs, Sibyl Birling is her husband's social superior and therefore represents the upper class and their attitudes. Priestley uses her as a reminder of the old world – a remnant of the Victorian era which conflicts with the emerging ideals of the younger generation. At "about fifty" in 1912, Sibyl has grown up and been moulded within the ideologies of the Victorian era: she is shown to have a lack of interest in alcohol, exude authority over those she deems beneath her (i.e. Edna and Inspector Goole), and is exposed for her "cold-hearted" attitude towards Eva Smith's illegitimate pregnancy and dire state of destitution. She retains her distanced and unemotional façade throughout the play, proud and prejudiced against the lower classes.

Like her husband, Mrs Birling demands respect and authority from everyone. She often comments on the "impertinence" of others, particularly Eva Smith. She conjures images of a strict school teacher from whom the audience would not want a telling-off! She presents as the archetypal socialite, running her household with the efficiency of a military general and engaging in activities which were deemed appropriate for her social standing, such as her work with the women's charity. Her disdain for the Inspector is not something she attempts to hide, entering "*self-confidently*" and talking to him "*rather-grandly*" about his methods. Despite demanding respect and authority in her own right, Mrs Birling also demonstrates on several occasions how she defers to her husband in accordance with the patriarchal customs of the time, telling the children that they must "be quiet so that your father can decide what we ought to do". She takes no trouble asserting her authority even over her children, often chastising their behaviour, their phrases and belittling them with words such as "child," despite their attempts to dissuade her from making mistakes.

Mrs Birling is one of the most stalwart characters in rejecting culpability. She stands by what she sees as her "duty" to refuse aid to Eva Smith, as she judged her to have "ridiculous airs." Through this, Priestley demonstrates the internalised superiority of the upper Edwardian classes and how this impacts their interactions with others. Her damnation of the father of Eva Smith's comes back to haunt her in the form of her own son, cracking her façade and leaving her "*frightened*" and "*agitated*" – a far cry from the stoic Victorian matriarch we met at the beginning. This is why she is so delighted when Gerald exposes the investigation as a hoax and they discover no girl has been brought to the infirmary as a suicide, finding the whole thing "amusing" instead. Through her character, Priestley openly critiques archaic values and prejudices, condemning the class divide and way it impedes any form of social responsibility or generosity.

Sheila Birling

Sheila is arguably the most interesting character within the play as she evolves into a completely different person by the time the curtains close. When the audience is first introduced to her, she is exactly as described in the stage directions: *"very pleased with life and rather excited."* Her engagement to the charismatic, wealthy, and handsome Gerald is the **epitome** of what every young upper class woman was encouraged to desire in the Edwardian period: with no ability to undertake a profession, or have any freedom to make decisions about her life, choosing to marry Gerald and gain more social standing is exactly what Sheila would have been told would make her happy. Sheila is shown to have materialistic tendencies from the outset, firstly through her admiration of her engagement ring, and subsequently in the trip to Millward's which proves devastating for Eva Smith. Priestley presents her as vain and self-indulgent, playing into the stereotype of a young upper-class woman of the Edwardian era.

Epitome: the perfect example of something.

The more vindictive aspects of her personality give rise to her jealousy of Eva Smith and her attempt to get her fired from Milward's. When faced with the consequences of her actions, Sheila confronts the uncomfortable truth about how her actions affected someone else's life and uses this as an opportunity to mature and change. She proceeds to try and stop her loved ones from making things worse for themselves with their coldness about the situation. She is one of the only characters (aside from Eric) who truly understands the deep severity of what their collective actions have caused: the suicide of another human being. She constantly calls on the older generation to not forget or dismiss the impact of the evening's events, critiquing them for "pretending everything's just as it was before," but to no avail.

Sheila is the most affected by the Inspector's visit: throughout the play, the audience watches as she becomes more assertive and morally aware, changing from a materialistic and self-focused girl to a conscious and free-thinking young woman. She is aware of the devastating effect her family's prejudice and apathy has caused, using the violent imagery of the role "to hang ourselves" to demonstrate how gravely she sees their situation. She constantly demonstrates empathy and her increasing self-awareness and emotional intelligence contrast with her parents' denial and arrogance. Her ideals of superiority and nonchalance are stripped away and she begins to think freely about not only Eva Smith but society as a whole, critiquing the apathy of others, symbolising social consciousness and change. Although her parents do not internalise her wise words, the audience certainly does, as Priestly positions us to empathise with Sheila in her journey of acquiring empathy and a broader perspective.

Eric Birling

Prodigal: wasting money on extravagances; comes from the Biblical story of the prodigal son who spends his father's money but returns to seek forgiveness.

Eric Birling is the textbook **prodigal** son: he drinks to excess, spends his father's money, shirks responsibility, and exhibits erratic behaviour. He is a young man of upper-middle class origin with links to a prosperous business – he should have the world at his feet. Yet Priestley reveals that Eric is "not quite at ease," and he appears out of place within the supposed serenity of the Birling household. Eric is characterised as a mostly silent observer or wallflower. There is something enigmatic about him, simultaneously a product of his middle class upbringing but also a staunch supporter of Eva Smith throughout the questioning. He asks questions about why the lower classes should not campaign for higher wages, and comments on his family's disastrous actions towards her.

Eric is often used as the proverbial punching bag by his father, with almost everything he says being met with rejection or contempt which highlights the distance in their relationship, further exemplified when Eric openly states he cannot be truthful with his father because of his lack of compassion. His mother is seen to both berate and infantilise him, ignorant of the depths of his drinking habit and shocked when she learns of his immoral behaviour. Whilst he and Sheila argue much like any siblings, he supports her as she attempts to rally the others to change.

Eric's actions towards Eva Smith are one of the final nails in her coffin. He is shown to have badly mistreated her, demonstrating a misogyny and carelessness which ultimately ends in her pregnancy. Their first interaction is left ambiguous as to whether or not it was consensual, with Eric revealing that he was applying pressure on her to sleep with him due to his alcohol consumption. Through this, Priestley exposes Eric's most dangerous flaws and critiques this flagrant disrespect for women, thereby demonstrating the effects of toxic masculinity and misogyny. Furthermore, Eric sees stealing money to help Eva Smith as justified as it is in service of helping someone in need, further distancing himself from the politics of his parents. His moral compass is one of the strongest within the play and, by the fall of the curtain, Eric has matured emotionally and ethically, showing hope for a more compassionate and responsible society, even though he remains an imperfect and culpable character.

Gerald Croft

Gerald symbolises the upper class aristocracy. Heir to a title and a prosperous competitor of Mr Birling, he is the typical respectable man-about-town and an ideal candidate for Sheila to marry. He is suave and charming from the outset, polite to each member of the Birling family. He is shown to agree with many of Mr Birling's beliefs, is cordial to Mrs Birling, tender with Sheila, and friendly but indifferent to Eric. His alliance with Mr Birling continues throughout the investigations, highlighting his support for the values of the capitalist society that has enabled them both to thrive.

However, Gerald's image as the romantic 'hero' is shattered when the Inspector begins to question him about Eva Smith, whom he knew as Daisy Renton. During their affair, he provided her with shelter and money and, while he claims he genuinely cared for her, he is revealed to have ended the relationship when it became inconvenient. By portraying this abandonment alongside Eric's treatment of Eva Smith, Priestley further exposes the abhorrent treatment of women by men who view them as romantic conquests. Gerald's duplicity in hiding this affair from Sheila also plays upon the motif of truth and how, like the other characters, the truth of who Gerald really is behind closed doors is hidden by the expectations of honour and chivalry associated with the superiority of his birth and rank.

Gerald is the first to question the credibility of Inspector Goole, arguably as a way to deflect attention from his own guilt. Like the elder Birlings, he is relieved when the evening is revealed to be a "hoax." He believes that, now he has uncovered the truth, the equilibrium can be restored and he can still marry Sheila. Through Gerald, Priestley explores the moral ambiguity of those who appear respectable but act selfishly.

Inspector Goole

Inspector Goole is the cornerstone for the action in the play, without whom none of the characters' secrets would be revealed. He is the personification of conscience and guilt: he forces everyone else to confront how they failed Eva Smith, persisting in his line of enquiry to the point that each character has to accept their responsibility. Priestley shows how the Inspector commands the scenes, often returning the warring family to the issue at hand: the girl's death. He exhibits impressive skills in **rhetoric**, using the words of others to expose their prejudices and elicit feelings of guilt.

Rhetoric: the art of effective writing or speaking, especially when employing persuasive language.

Despite being of a different class to the Birlings, Inspector Goole is a domineering figure who "*creates at once an impression of massiveness, solidity and purposefulness.*" This stoic and powerful presence grounds all of the action that will take place during the following acts, forcing the characters to confront reality despite their sometimes emotional or dismissive reactions. As a policeman, the Inspector is technically lower class and therefore Mr Birling's inferior; however, through Priestley's description, the audience is led to understand that it is Inspector Goole who now commands the room. His presence is irrefutable, immediately shifting the power balance onstage and perhaps even making us reconsider what authority means in this play. He stands out in stark contrast to the other characters, speaking "*carefully, weightily*" and makes no qualms about ruffling some feathers, with his "*disconcerting habit of looking hard at the person he addresses before actually speaking*". His job through the play is to uncover the truth by whatever means necessary: he is forceful without being overly pushy, patiently and methodically interrogating each suspect and extracting their confession. Priestley positions him as the foil to Mr Birling, juxtaposing Goole's socialist views on collective responsibility with Mr Birling's capitalist ideology of every man having to "look after himself and his own." Through this, the audience is shown contrasting political ideas in dialogue and personified on the stage, thereby deepening the understanding of the Edwardian political landscape.

Whilst characters like Arthur, Mrs Birling, and Gerald rebuke the Inspector, Sheila, and Eric appear to mature and evolve due to his investigation, agreeing with his sentiments and attempting to get the older generation to change their ways. Through them, Priestley represents the changing attitudes of the early 20th century and discredits the outdated system through which families such as the Birlings have made their fortune and in turn lost touch with their humanity, forgetting their responsibility to their fellow man. Ultimately, Priestley doesn't provide the audience an answer as to who the Inspector was. Is he the personification of conscience? Is he an innocent bystander seeking to do good? Is he a spokesperson for Priestley himself inserted into the play to warn future generations about the consequences of selfishness? It almost doesn't matter: the spine-chilling final message Inspector Goole delivers, with humanity learning responsibility through "fire and blood and anguish," invoking the horrors of World Wars and atrocities of history, transcends the importance of defining his character.

Eva Smith

Arguably the most important character within the play, we never see or hear from Eva Smith herself. As such, she is a construct used by Priestley to represent the everyday man or woman: a humble member of the working class just trying to survive in a system not made to support them. To me, she is reminiscent of Daphne Du Maurier's Mrs de Winter from the novel *Rebecca*: they are both women who are stripped of autonomy in one way or another. Whilst the reader never learns the real name of Mrs De Winter, the audience is never allowed to meet Eva Smith due to the callous actions of the characters onstage, thereby evidencing her limited power in her own life.

Her name is important within the construction of the text: 'Eva' is reminiscent of the Biblical Eve, the first woman, and therefore symbolises humanity and the consequences of actions. Secondly, the surname 'Smith' is very common in the United Kingdom, establishing her as a representation of the average, working-class person. Priestley also utilises Eva Smith to evoke sympathy from the audience: many of the characters comment that she was "very pretty" with a "nice little promising life," demonstrating the tragedy of her death as her potential was never realised. Her lack of independence and reliance on the whims of others exposes the harsh realities of the class system, never being able to fully control the course of her life: having lost both parents and subsequently moving to Brumley, she relies on employment by businessmen such as Mr Birling. Reliance is something that Eva Smith has to submit to throughout her life, having to then rely upon Gerald when she is "desperately hard up" and literally going hungry. Her "lonely" existence is interspersed with unfortunate meetings with the characters in the play, as the audience sees her life slowly disintegrate. We are powerless to help and simply have to bear witness to the tales of her misfortunes. Whether she is a single figure or a combination of any of the girls who have suffered at the hands of the other characters, her death holds each person accountable for their greed, apathy, and selfishness, encouraging the audience to reflect on how their own actions may impact others.

Edna

Though a small part within the scope of the text, Edna's character is important to consider. She is the parlour maid who clears the dinner after the family's celebration and is therefore the representation of the working servant class within the play. Through the hierarchical structure of countless generations, the notion of a serving class had evolved from the concept of unpaid serfdom of the medieval period. Serfdom was an early form of subservience, where those who worked and lived on land owned by someone else were subject to their will and word. Evolving to the image of service we associate with later generations, men, women, and children of lower means were employed to look after wealthy aristocratic families, with many born to families in service following their parents' footsteps and staying in service their entire lives. In situating his play in an upper-middle class home, Priestley uses the character of Edna to represent this section of Edwardian society. Every time Edna addresses Mr or Mrs Birling, she shows her subservience by addressing them as "Sir" and "Ma'am," whereas she is simply "Edna." Through this, Priestley subtly acclimatises the audience to the class system and the respect Mr and Mrs Birling are used to receiving. Whilst it was common to refer to others with the titles of Mr, Mrs, or Miss (or with their ranking titles), many servants were referred to by their given first names, thereby demonstrating the power imbalance at play within the text.

Section 5

Key Themes Analysis

Class

An intrinsic element of the play, Priestley's exploration of the Edwardian class system through a pro-socialist lens exposes the rigidities and inequities of this time period. Writing from a post-war perspective, Priestley plays upon his audience's knowledge of the unravelling of Edwardian structures, such as the gaping divide between upper and lower class, as a result of both world conflicts. His characters are intentionally prejudiced and ignorant of the struggles of the working class in order to highlight the effects of class division.

Whilst the characters can portray and exhibit sympathy for Eva Smith on a basic level, when drawn into her story, characters like Mr and Mrs Birling attempt to construct a "wall" to keep their distance from her: this wall represents the divide between upper and working class people, dictating how each group could live their lives and what was expected of them. They are unable to fully empathise with the plight of working class individuals because they have never experienced an unprivileged life: they have never lived through poverty, a lack of education, or a lack of opportunities. This results in an absence of understanding when presented with a character like Eva Smith, who is denied dignity and seen as an inconvenience simply for asking for basic human necessities. Her attempts to better her life and fight for better wages are seen as an inconvenience to Mr Birling, who calls their strike a "pitiful affair" not because it conjures pity for their circumstance, but because they were never going to be taken seriously. By starkly depicting the apathy of the upper classes, Priestly exposes the consequences of the established class system in creating distance and disharmony between members of society who, in his opinion, should be treated with equal respect and care.

Furthermore, the class system's inherent moral hierarchy is exposed by Priestley as a façade: through his characters, he demonstrates how these characters are occupied with maintaining respectability and social status whilst behaving in morally questionable behaviour. Although appearing to be the "respectable citizens" so valued by Edwardian society, each character exhibits traits which undermine this assumed morality: Mr Birling's greed results in the unfair dismissal of a worker whom he does not consider worth his investment; Sheila's vanity also results in a petty, unfair dismissal; Gerald's ignorance perpetuates a lack of stability and safety, Eric's naivety gives rise to her pregnancy and furthered loneliness; and Mrs Birling's cruelty is the final nail in her coffin – Eva Smith pays the ultimate price for the actions of others.

Each character is, in some way, hiding the distasteful aspects of their true nature from the audience, wearing the "evening-dress" of the time and performing a respectability which is demolished through the evening. The Inspector unveils the hypocrisy of their illusions through his blunt questioning, challenging their self-perceptions and proposing a different way of life to benefit every member of society. Whilst it is arguable that the Inspector's true identity is the great question of the text, he never hides his true character from the audience: inquisitive, commanding and forward. His morality is the aspect of his character which cannot be questioned and is never hidden, unlike the other characters.

Ultimately, class is one of the cornerstones of *An Inspector Calls*, influencing how these characters behave and interact, driving Priestley's call for social equality. Through the presentation of this conflict, Priestley allows audiences of any period to understand the intricacies of Edwardian class politics and stereotypes, as well as universal and timeless notions like the importance of caring for others.

Old vs. young

In the play's context of social, political, and cultural turmoil, ideologies which had been upheld and uninterrupted for generations were being challenged throughout the British population. Priestley encapsulates these evolving attitudes through his portrayal of the conflict between the older and younger generations within *An Inspector Calls*.

The generational divide is evident from the outset of the play. Whilst it is noted that their social backgrounds differ, Mr and Mrs Birling are shown to be aligned and united in their social views. They have benefited from the capitalist system and have no desire to see their way of life changed. Mr Birling's staunch commitment to individualism is unwavering and, when paired with Mrs Birling's abuse of position within her committee, demonstrates their primary concern being with their own and status. They do not condone any challenges to the accepted order of society, attempting to assuage and placate both Sheila and the Inspector whenever they are confronted with the consequences of this unjust system. Their inflexibility to even consider or attempt to change their behaviour emphasises their ignorance of the consequences of their actions. Priestley uses their rigidity and denial of culpability to show his audience why privileged people within society may wish to uphold the system which benefits them, whilst also conveying the impact this has on those who suffer as a result.

In direct contrast to the older generation, Priestley's depiction of the younger characters within the play addresses his hope for the future and the possibility of change. Sheila and Eric are paradoxes to their parents: although they have benefited from an upbringing within a house of wealth and privilege, they are not anywhere near as close-minded as their parents. When confronted with the visceral reality of Eva Smith's suicide and how their actions were the cause of such horrors, the siblings are immediately remorseful. Sheila, in particular, shows moral growth and acceptance from her previous materialistic and self-absorbed mindset, drawing attention to her father's inability to see his female workers as "people" and not just "cheap labour." She continuously highlights, through her emotional connection to Eva Smith, the apathy of her parents, reflecting Priestley's message of social equality and connectivity.

Eric's journey in the play is similar to his sister and it is shown that he is susceptible to the Inspector's teachings. He questions his father's morality and beliefs early on in the play with regards to the worker's strike and is shown to be devastated by his part in Eva Smith's death. He relates to his sister's fear within the final act after seeing his parents return to their ignorant ways, thereby indicating the possibility that they will both proceed to live more morally aware and just lives.

Through the contrast of the older generations' immovable prejudice with the malleability of the younger generation, Priestley proposes a hope for a more compassionate and equal future. The utter upheaval of the First World War and its effect on not only the class system but voting rights, the density of the younger generation and other aspects of society is something that Priestley's audience would be aware of. In the landscape of a shaken post-war Britain, this evolution of attitudes and a reshuffling of societal frameworks was entirely possible.

Representation of women

There is significant focus within the play on the lives of women within the early 20th century. Through the female characters, Priestley critiques the misogyny of the period and its effect upon women's positions and place within society. It is evident in the text that the women are seen as social inferiors: despite being of a higher social background than her husband, Mrs Birling defers to his decisions and upholds him as the head of the household, positioning herself as almost a passive bystander in her own life. Likewise, Sheila's life is reduced to her status as a and prospective wife, only gaining a voice by distancing herself from the attitudes of others, specifically her father and fiancé. Whilst their upper class position does allow them some comfort, it is ultimately Eva Smith's position in the working class which fully highlights the limitations of women. She is completely at the mercy of others, often men, for survival and is dehumanised when refused fair working wages. She is called a "wretched girl" and viewed as a troublemaker for standing up for equality. Priestley conveys the impacts of patriarchal attitudes within his contemporary society, exposing the imbalance between the sexes and their freedoms, thereby highlighting the need for more progressive attitudes towards equality.

Priestely also presents the discourse surrounding internalised misogyny, whereby women are influenced by patriarchal ideology and thereby contribute to the oppression of their own sex. This is most evident through Mrs Birling's character, both in her relationship with her own daughter and her cruelty towards Eva Smith. What begins as motherly berating of Sheila descends into a **vitriolic** dismissal and critique of her character, noting she is "hysterical" and "childish." By playing upon ideas of women as inferior and infantile, Mrs Birling upholds and perpetuates misogynistic attitudes

Vitriolic: hateful, spiteful.

Her judgement of other women is exemplified through her role on the women's committee: it would be assumed that, in this position, Mrs Birling would provide sympathetic care and help to women most in need. Priestley flips this notion on its head, however, as she shows his audience how Mrs Birling abuses her position to reject Eva Smith's claim, hiding behind a façade of respectability and moral superiority. Her judgement of women like Eva Smith, who have been subjected to begging for help due to their desperation and lowly status, highlights how women can be culpable in the continuation of patriarchal control and attitudes towards women and their sexuality.

Through Eva Smith's sexual relationships, Priestley further illustrates the objectification of women and how upper class men often mistreated working class women. Gerald's affair is easily ended because he holds all of the power and simply discards her when she becomes inconvenient. His image of himself as her protector, her "fairy prince," communicates the patronising attitude of women as inferior and in need of male protection rather than free human beings. Eric, in turn, treats her as "the end of a stupid drunken evening" with little care for her own feelings. She is often described by the other characters as "pretty" before anything else, conveying how she is reduced to only her physical appearance. Through the implicit mentions of the Palace Bar, it is suggested that she may have been working as a prostitute, thereby further demonstrating how she has been objectified and compelled to engage in what her society would have regarded as immoral behaviour in order to sustain herself. Thus, the women Priestley presents are shown to be at the mercy of men and the patriarchal society which diminished their worth, regardless of class, exposing the inequalities of the Edwardian and post-war eras.

Collective vs. individual responsibility

One of the main elements in socialist doctrine is the notion of collectivity. It calls for social rather than private ownership, and promotes community as a way of achieving an equal society where there are no hierarchies. Whilst the political landscape of Britain was changing drastically during the Second World War, with the Labour Party ascending to government in 1945, many still opposed the ideals of socialism in favour of the previously Conservative government. Indications of the nation's desire for reform through the years leading up to this election provide a springboard from which playwrights such as Priestley could begin to present stories which echo the thoughts of a changing society. Rather than upholding the class system and unfair division of wealth which saw many living in poverty, Priestley uses *An Inspector Calls* to call for a rebuilding of society based on ideals of equality and collective responsibility. The conflict of these two ideas is presented throughout the play, personified through Mr Birling and Inspector Goole. The two characters are shown to clash almost from their meeting, voicing the ethics of both principles and demonstrating their juxtaposing attitudes.

Mr Birling is the voice of self-interest, seeing social equality as a threat to his way of life and the status quo which has benefited him and his family. His speech to Eric and Gerald advocates explicitly for individualism, rejecting the notions of fellowship and community: "A man has to mind his own business and look after himself and his own." He is an example of the "hard-headed businessman" who's greed and quest for control affects the lives of those who work for him, those who must obey his rules in order to simply provide for their families. He is so far removed from the **quotidian** existence of his fellow man that he is unable to find any common ground with those like Eva Smith who need very little to improve their standard of living. He does not care for the opinions of those he sees as inferior, often protesting whenever an opposing idea he is faced with, declaring it "nonsense" and those who speak it "cranks." He prioritises personal growth and wealth over his social duty, ultimately being reminded that his status within the community is not simply a title without consequences: "Public men, Mr Birling, have responsibilities as well as privileges." This summarises the negative effect that a capitalist way of thinking has had upon men like Mr Birling, as he forgets the real purpose of those in power: helping and caring for those less fortunate. Through his opening comments on the events of the time, notably the "unsinkable" Titanic and the "silly little war scares" on the impending outbreak of the First World War, highlight his total lack of awareness and making him a character the audience cannot see themselves in.

Quotidian: normal, everyday, routine.

Inspector Goole is the dramatic **foil** to Mr Birling: where one covets wealth and position, the other seeks truth and equality. The Inspector is the personification of socialist ideology, conveying the message for social reform. He meticulously deconstructs the Birling family's understanding of their places in society and, by confronting them with the calamitous consequences of their behaviour, forces them and the audience to consider how they might change their ways. He literally brings each character together through the "chain of events" which resulted in Eva Smith's death, demonstrating the link between every member of humanity.

Foil: a character who contrasts with another, used by the author to differentiate or emphasise their differences.

His role in the text is not simply to investigate the tragic death of a tragic figure, but to educate the characters and the audience on the merits of interconnectivity. He is the mouthpiece through which Priestley critiques selfishness and the apathy of the privileged classes, bringing the consequences of their immorality straight to their front door. The name "Goole" is reminiscent of ghoul, hinting at his enigmatic character from his introduction, implying a supernatural element to him. He is literally seen to haunt the Birlings and Gerald Croft; he is the **manifestation** of their guilt, demonstrating the power of moral culpability.

Manifestation: the physical embodiment or proof of something.

Priestley therefore implores his audience to face the realities of their own society, one driven by individual desire rather than collective unity. His presentation of this theme is central to the driving action of the text, using the Birling family as an symbol for the privileged few, and taking the audience, both contemporary and modern, on a journey through which they can learn the values of collective responsibility.

Loss of innocence

Whilst not one of the most visible themes within the text, multiple characters go through a process of losing their innocence. It is intrinsically related to the moral growth of the younger characters, Sheila and Eric, as they are introduced to the harsh realities of their society, as well as to Eva Smith who loses her innocence at the hands of misogynistic men and the brutal consequences of capitalist individualism.

Sheila's evolution within the text serves as the clearest presentation of this theme: through losing her innocence, Sheila regains her autonomy and begins to show signs of being a responsible and empathetic member of society. When the audience first meets Sheila, her naivety and affection for her parents is evident through calling them "Daddy" and "Mummy," whilst she is treated like a child by them, evidently doted on and admired for her gentility and femininity. She spars with Eric, belittling him and exhibiting behaviours common with a childish sibling dynamic. The discovery that she had a part to play in Eva Smith's death is the catalyst for Sheila's loss of innocence: her metaphorical blinkers are removed and she begins to see the true nature of the world, understanding for the first time how her actions may negatively impact someone else's life. Unlike her parents, Sheila's reaction of horror is genuine and empathetic as she "almost breaks down" when realising how superficial and jealous her behaviour was, distancing her from their example of moral superficiality. She takes full responsibility for her actions, removing any guilt from Eva Smith, explicitly acknowledging "it was my own fault." By the end of the play, Sheila talks to her parents as "Father" and "Mother," highlighting her emergence into womanhood. She is the most enlightened character, actively begging the others to see the error of their ways and to accept the desperate and immediate need to change. She is no longer hidden from the truth of her society, the undeniable suffering she herself has had a part in inflicting, and represents the hope and ability to take control of our own morality.

Eric, in turn, also undergoes his own loss of innocence. When he is first introduced, he is an immature and reckless young man who's excessive drinking appears to be the largest flaw to his character. When it is revealed, however, that he thoughtlessly carried out an affair with Eva Smith, he struggles to understand the gravity of his circumstance, attempting to make amends by stealing money and thus making him a figure of moral ambiguity.

The audience sees that, like his sister, Eric's privileged upbringing has shielded him from taking accountability and the very real consequences that come from selfish and harmful behaviour. He is equally as horrified by his behaviour as Sheila was with hers, "*miserably*" recounting the details to the Inspector. Through his acceptance and repentance, Eric demonstrates that these tragic events have resulted in his own loss of innocence, leaving him a more responsible man capable of moral growth. He is no longer the "young fool" his father views him as, but a character who exhibits the ability we all have to change our ways, something which would never have been achievable without the loss of his innocence.

Eva Smith's character is also highly relevant to the theme of lost innocence. Whilst she is a character who inherently understands the reality of Edwardian society, her innocence is compromised through her dismissal from Millward's, as she is forced to become Daisy Renton, "with other ideas." Through her presence at the Palace Bar, it is suggested that she ultimately turns to a life of prostitution and depending upon the generosity of others, thereby losing her innocence and autonomy. By presenting Eva Smith's loss of innocence, Priestley provides representation for the countless women who, through the recklessness of others, have been forced to endure hardships and dangerous situations, encouraging sympathy from his audience. Ultimately, Priestley's investigation of this theme highlights the inequalities of society, conveying how the younger characters are awoken to their moral responsibilities and the possibility for social reform that this brings, thereby critiquing the complacency and ignorance of the established order.

Duty and truth

Inextricable: tied together in a way that can't easily be undone.

Ideas of truth and duty are **inextricable** within *An Inspector Calls*. At the heart of this text is a search for the truth: the truth of each character's relationship to Eva Smith, the truth about why she decided to end her own life, the truth about Inspector Goole's identity and intentions, and ultimately the truth of moral responsibility. The Inspector disrupts the Birlings' celebration and does not leave until he uncovers each detail about their stories, and how they ultimately contributed to her tragic death. Often the characters hide behind their well-to-do façade, or behind the social conventions they believe will keep them safe: Mr Birling, when threatened, attempts to dissuade his questioning by making reference to his connection with the Chief of Police: "Perhaps I ought to warn you that he's an old friend of mine,and that I see him fairly frequently." Playing once again with power dynamics, Birling attempts to use his standing in society to hinder the investigation, or at least to coerce the Inspector into backing down. Each time the characters are questioned, they are made to confront the truth that they have failed in their moral duty to another member of society, simply because she was an inconvenience or challenged an individual's sense of self.

It is not only the truth about Eva Smith's death that is at play within the text, but the truth behind each of these seemingly respectable characters. Although Gerald declares that they are all "respectable citizens and not criminals," Inspector Goole's following statement is what the audience is encouraged to consider by the end: "Sometimes there isn't as much difference as you'd think. Often, if it was left to me, I wouldn't know where to draw the line." Through the interrogations, the characters reveal things about themselves that exposes the true nature of their personalities – aspects they have not until this moment considered to be harmful. Where Mr and Mrs Birling attempt to cling to social stereotypes and the aspects of upper class impartiality which have traditionally allowed them to remain detached from others, Sheila and Eric develop keener understandings of their moral responsibility through their acceptance of the truth, offering audiences some hope in this representation of the next generation.

The concept of "duty" is explored in detail within the text as a tool through which Priestley presents the ideas of community and ethical responsibility. The notion of an intrinsic responsibility to carry out is held by several characters, such as Mrs Birling. She sees it as her "duty" to refuse Eva Smith aid, on the grounds of her supposed "impertinence" when, in reality, she abuses her position to influence the decision of the committee simply because she didn't like how she had been spoken to, highlighting how her duty can be overlooked when her personal comfort is threatened. She then presses the Inspector to publicly reprimand the father of Eva Smith's unborn child, saying "I consider it your duty," ignorant of the knowledge that this "chief culprit" is her own son. Her dedication to this notion of duty could culminate in the ruin of the family, and is something to be avoided at all costs. Mr Birling's duty as a "public man," displaying his various roles within Brumley as a badge of honour, is shown to be juxtaposed by his treatment of his workers as "cheap labour," showing how his duty to his employees is often overlooked in favour of financial gain. The duty which Priestley asks his audience to accept is that we have to look out for our fellow man, to recognise the impact that we have on the lives of others, and how living by this ideal will create a more just equilibrium.

Priestley demonstrates that ignoring our duty to one another and refusing to face the truth about ourselves and the world in which we live can have catastrophic consequences, both for ourselves morally and for those around us.

Section 6

Structural Features Analysis

Three act structure

Split into three acts, *An Inspector Calls* has a very clear beginning, middle, and end. Whilst a fairly common structure for theatre, this allows Priestly to introduce and explore all of the characters and themes at play, culminating in a final act where characters are changed (or not changed) and have to come to terms with what has unfolded. The three act structure also lends itself to being performed with no interval: although each act ends with a cliff-hanger, the action carries on without interruption. The continuous nature of the text allows the events of the play to unfold in real-time, giving the audience the chance to go on their journey with each character and simultaneously experience everything that they experience onstage, making their discoveries with them.

Motifs and symbols

The telephone and calls

The multitude of calls within the text are the symbolic triggers for action, interrupting the equilibrium and creating a space for the truth to come to the forefront. Through the calls, the outside world seeps into the world of the play: whilst the theatre has often been used as a medium of escapism, this allows Priestley to remind the audience that they are subject to the same moral responsibilities as the characters onstage. They are not allowed to forget their lives and their realities, instead being confronted with universal decisions and behaviours, re-affirming that there are "millions and millions of Eva Smiths and John Smiths" and that this scenario could happen to anyone.

The Inspector's physical call acts as the catalyst for the play's action to unfold: without this visit, the characters in the text may never have been forced to confront their moral failings. The group is 'called' to answer for their behaviour, called almost to a metaphorical witness stand where they must recount their past and face the reality of what their actions have brought into being. Truth is revealed through the telephone calls, symbolic of a modern and innovative world which can be juxtaposed with the archaic and insular behaviour of the upper classes. The calls again link the dining-room scene to the outside world: both Mr Birling and Gerald make calls in order to establish the truth, confirming whether the Inspector was a real police officer and whether a girl had died by suicide in the infirmary. At the end of the play, having dismissed the evening as a hoax, Mr Birling receives a final call on the telephone, disrupting the order once more, and learns a new inspector is about to arrive following the real death of a young girl. Through his dramatic twist, Priestley emphasises the inescapable nature of truth and reality, with the private lives of the characters once more infiltrated by their social and moral responsibility.

Alcohol

Throughout the text, alcohol consumption is a recurring motif. The play begins with the family drinking, making a toast to Sheila and Gerald's engagement. The champagne they have had during dinner and the port they use afterwards for the toast references their desire to celebrate the evening. There is even a suggestion that Mrs Birling doesn't drink as much as the others, with Mr Birling having to persuade her as it is a "special occasion." This again plays into the Victorian ideals of sobriety, something the upper-class Sibyl clearly adheres to. During the play, however, it becomes clear that Eric is a much heavier drinker than the rest of the characters. At the opening, he is silent until he abruptly laughs, leading Sheila to surmise that he is "squiffy." When it is revealed later that Eric has a drinking problem, his mother is shocked by the revelation and her disapproval is evident, speaking to Sheila "bitterly," as if resentful for being told the truth. Priestley also evidences the dangers of alcohol through Eric's interaction with Eva Smith: Eric admits that he was "in that state where a chap easily turns nasty," therefore critiquing not only the negative impacts of alcohol. Eric's excessive drinking highlights actions and events he'd rather forget, which is replicated when several of the characters charge their glasses upon the realisation that they've been "had" by the Inspector, forgetting the importance of what they've gone through and beginning to "pretend" again.

Rope/hanging

Though a very small mention, the motif of the rope is a significant one. The image of the noose to "hang" the Birlings is symbolic of judgement and guilt, the ultimate consequence to their actions. With the death penalty only abolished in the UK in 1965, this punishment for the most severe of crimes such as murder would be a known aspect of the judgment system within both the Edwardian and post-war contexts of this play. It also acts as a physical link, much like the "chain of events," between Eva Smith and the other characters, something inescapable which they only worsen through their inability to accept their parts in her death. Sheila notes to her family that the Inspector is "giving us rope – so that we'll hang ourselves." This categorises him as the moral executioner, using the Birlings' own behaviour to confront them with their guilt, slowly tightening the vice of responsibility, one by one, as he carries out his exposing investigation. Ultimately, the family do hang themselves with their own actions with the final call confirming the death of a girl by suicide, unable to escape their moral responsibility and the consequences of their actions.

Rudeness

A recurring notion within the text, rudeness is used as a motif by Priestley to critique social expectations and etiquette and reinforce the themes of responsibility and community. Mr Birling often patronises the Inspector and is dismissive of the working class, revealing his arrogance and capitalist mindset. Mrs Birling, in turn, whilst openly detesting "impudence," is rude in her cold and distanced attitude towards others, often condescending in her tone. Her deep-rooted class prejudice towards characters like Eva Smith, calling her a girl "of that class," evidences her lack of empathy and judgmental attitude.

The motif is one of the ways in which Priestley explores the hypocrisy of the Birlings: the family pride themselves on their respectability whilst ultimately concealing actions of disrespect, cruelty and ignorance. Where the family view Inspector Goole's directness as rude, his blunt approach to his investigation purposefully uncovers the truth and forces the family to confront their actions. He refuses to obey the traditional power structures, inverting what is expected of him and challenging the assumed entitlement of the upper class elite. Through this motif, Priestley advocates for social change, highlighting the façade of etiquette within the class divide.

The engagement ring

Sheila's engagement ring symbolises not only romantic love within the play, but the materialism of the upper classes. When first given the ring, Sheila is in awe of its beauty and becomes fixated upon it, calling it "perfect." Indeed, both the ring and Sheila at this point represent the epitome of what women in the Edwardian period were expected to desire: marriage to a wealthy, handsome man of a prominent social standing. After the revelations of Sheila and Gerald's interactions with Eva Smith, Sheila calls off their engagement and returns the ring to Gerald. The ring, and by extension the idealism of marriage, has been tainted by the truth of their characters and their actions. Sheila sees this more clearly than Gerald, noting that "you and I aren't the same people who sat down to dinner here." In the final section of the play, Gerald (having convinced Mr and Mrs Birling that the whole evening was a hoax) attempts to give Sheila the ring back, saying "Everything's alright now," but Sheila refuses, telling him it's "too soon." Whilst to Gerald the ring is now returned to its original status, Sheila (having matured) now rejects this symbol of materialism and control.

Disinfectant

It is no coincidence that Priestley chooses swallowing disinfectant as Eva Smith's method of suicide. Typically used as a cleaning product, this conjures associations with cleanliness and sanitized objects. The tragedy of this image is simply that, in the eyes of Edwardian society, Eva Smith has become 'unclean' through her affairs and illegitimate pregnancy. By this logic, the disinfectant she swallows should restore her to her original purity; however, instead it destroys her in the most brutal and painful way.

The Titanic

The "unsinkable" Titanic is mentioned only briefly at the start of the play, but is important nonetheless. As previously mentioned, the dramatic irony of Mr Birling openly praising this feat of ingenuity will never be lost on an audience who knows the fate of the Titanic's maiden voyage. The ship can also however arguably be seen as a symbol for the destructive nature of capitalism: the catastrophic loss of life when the Titanic sank was partially due to the lack of lifeboats on board the ship, as the ships' owners deemed it displeasing and not in-keeping with the aesthetic to have the decks littered with lifeboats. Even in this small way, Priestly is subtly demonstrating a contempt for the capitalist way of life and thinking which governed both the Edwardian and post-war era.

Section 7

Quote Bank

Class

Quote	Character	Act
"All five are in evening dress of the period, the men in tails and white ties, not dinner-jackets."	Stage directions	Act One
"...her husband's social superior."	Stage directions	Act One
"She comes from an old country family – landed people and so forth – so it's only natural."	Mr Birling	Act One
"...so long as we behave ourselves, don't get into the police court or start a scandal – eh?"	Mr Birling	Act One
"...this is Mr Gerald Croft – the son of Sir George Croft – you know, Crofts Limited?"	Mr Birling	Act One
"I was an alderman for years – and Lord Mayor two years ago – and I'm still on the Bench..."	Mr Birling	Act One
"It's my duty to keep labour costs down... We were paying the usual rates and if they didn't like those rates, they could go and work somewhere else."	Mr Birling	Act One
"Rubbish! If you don't come down sharply on some of these people, they'd soon be asking for the earth."	Mr Birling	Act One
"Perhaps I ought to warn you that he's an old friend of mine..."	Mr Birling	Act One
"There are a lot of young women living that sort of existence in every city and big town in this country, Miss Birling. If there weren't the factories and warehouses wouldn't know where to look for cheap labour. Ask your father."	Inspector Goole	Act One
"After all, y'know, we're respectable citizens and not criminals"	Gerald Croft	Act One

“Sometimes there isn’t as much difference as you think.”	Inspector Goole	Act One
“And so you used the power you had... to punish the girl just because she made you feel like that?”	Inspector Goole	Act One
“Girls of that class...”	Mrs Birling	Act Two
“You mustn’t try to build up a kind of wall between us and that girl.”	Sheila Birling	Act Two
“You know of course that my husband was Lord Mayor only two years ago and that he’s still a magistrate...”	Mrs Birling	Act Two
“Women of the town?”	Mrs Birling	Act Two
“Alderman Meggarty? I must say, we *are* learning something tonight.”	Mrs Birling	Act Two
“I don’t think we want any further details of this disgusting affair...”	Mrs Birling	Act Two
“It means that we’ve no excuse now for putting on airs...”	Sheila Birling	Act Two
“We’ve done a great deal of useful work in helping deserving cases.”	Mrs Birling	Act Two
“...damned impudence!”	Mrs Birling	Act Two
“No I don’t. I know why she *needed* help.”	Inspector Goole	Act Two
“She was giving herself ridiculous airs. She was claiming elaborate fine feelings and scruples that were simply absurd in a girl in her position.”	Mrs Birling	Act Two
“Her position now is that she lies with a burnt-out inside on a slab.”	Inspector Goole	Act Two
“As if a girl of that sort would ever refuse money!”	Mrs Birling	Act Two
“You made her pay a heavy price for that...”	Inspector Goole	Act Three
“...and who here will suffer from that more than I will?”	Mr Birling	Act Three
“...with their lives, their hopes and fears, their suffering, and chance of happiness, all intertwined with our lives, with what we think and say and do.”	Inspector Goole	Act Three

Old vs. young

Quote	Character	Act
"But you youngsters just remember what I've said."	Mr Birling	Act One
"And we don't guess – we've had experience – and we *know*."	Mr Birling	Act One
"Why shouldn't try for higher wages? We try for the highest possible prices."	Eric Birling	Act One
"It's about time you learnt to face a few responsibilities."	Mr Birling	Act One
"You seem to have made a great impression on this child, Inspector."	Mrs Birling	Act Two
"We often do on the young ones. They're more impressionable."	Inspector Goole	Act Two
"Please don't contradict me like that."	Mrs Birling	Act Two
"He's only a boy."	Mrs Birling	Act Two
"What's the matter with that child?"	Mr Birling	Act Two
"And I'm not a child, don't forget. I have a right to know."	Sheila Birling	Act Two
"Silly boy!"	Mrs Birling	Act Two
"You're behaving like an hysterical child tonight."	Mrs Birling	Act Two
"If you'd any sense of loyalty..."	Mr Birling	Act Three
"Because you're not the kind of father a chap could go to when he's in trouble – that's why."	Eric Birling	Act Three
"Why, you hysterical young fool..."	Mr Birling	Act Three
"Eric, I'm absolutely ashamed of you."	Mrs Birling	Act Three
"...don't forget I'm ashamed of you as well – yes, both of you."	Eric Birling	Act Three
"Don't be childish, Sheila."	Mrs Birling	Act Three
"If you want to know, it's you two who are being childish – trying not to face the facts."	Sheila	Act Three

"Some fathers I know would have kicked you out of the house anyhow by this time. So hold your tongue if you want to stay here."	Mr Birling	Act Three
"...from the way you children talk..."	Mrs Birling	Act Three
"Now look at the pair of them – the famous younger generation who know it all. And they can't even take a joke"	Mr Birling	Act Three

Representation of women

Quote	Character	Act
"When you're married you'll realise that men with important work to do sometimes have to spend nearly all their time and energy on their business. You'll have to get used to it, just as I had."	Mrs Birling	Act One
"What an expression, Sheila. Really, the things you girls pick up these days."	Mrs Birling	Act One
"Oh – its wonderful! Look – Mummy – isn't it beauty?"	Sheila	Act One
"I think Sheila and I had better go into the drawing-room and leave you men"	Mrs Birling	Act One
"*Sheila is still admiring her ring*"	Stage directions	Act One
"You'd think a girl never had any clothes before she gets married. Women are potty about them."	Eric	Act One
"She'd had a lot to say – far too much – so she had to go."	Mr Birling	Act One
"Nothing to do with you, Sheila. Run along."	Mr Birling	Act One
"so you used the power you had, as a daughter of a good customer and also of a man well-known in the town, to punish the girl just because she made you feel like that?"	Inspector Goole	Act One
"And you think young women ought to be protected against unpleasant and disturbing things?"	Inspector Goole	Act Two
"Women of the town?"	Mrs Birling	Act Two
"I hate those hard-eyed dough-faced women."	Gerald	Act Two

"She looked young and fresh and charming and altogether out of place down there."	Gerald	Act Two
"she only escaped with a torn blouse."	Sheila	Act Two
"gave me a glance that was nothing less than a cry for help."	Gerald	Act Two
"I didn't ask for anything in return."	Gerald	Act Two
"She was a woman. She was lonely."	Inspector Goole	Act Two
"But I think she has only herself to blame."	Mrs Birling	Act Two
"You've had children. You must have known what she was feeling. And you slammed the door in her face."	Inspector Goole	Act Two
"She was giving herself ridiculous airs."	Mrs Birling	Act Two
"As if a girl of that sort would ever refuse money."	Mrs Birling	Act Two
"Be quiet Sheila!... You're behaving like an hysterical child tonight."	Mrs Birling	Act Two
"well, I was in that state where a man easily turns nasty."	Eric	Act Three
"I wasn't in love with her or anything – but I liked her – she was pretty and a good sport"	Eric	Act Three
"I hate these fat old tarts round the town"	Eric	Act Three
"She didn't want to marry me [...] In a way, she treated me – as if I were a kid."	Eric	Act Three
"Just used her for the end of a stupid drunken evening, as if she was an animal, a thing, not a person."	Inspector Goole	Act Three
"Don't be childish Sheila."	Mrs Birling	Act Three
"Now just be quiet so that you father can decide what we ought to do."	Mrs Birling	Act Three

Collective vs. individual responsibility

Quote	Character	Act
"a man has to make his own way"	Mr Birling	Act One
"But the way some of these cranks talk and write nowadays, you'd think everybody has to look after everybody else"	Mr Birling	Act One
"as if we were all mixed up together like bees in a hive – community and all that nonsense."	Mr Birling	Act One
"a man has to mind his own business and look after himself and his own"	Mr Birling	Act One
"what happened to her then may have determined what happened to her afterwards, and what happened to her afterwards may have driven her to suicide. A chain of events."	Inspector Goole	Act One
"If we were all responsible for everything that happened to everybody we'd had anything to do with, it would be very awkward, wouldn't it?"	Mr Birling	Act One
"these young women counting their pennies in their dingy little back bedrooms."	Inspector Goole	Act One
"A nice little promising life there, I thought, and a nasty mess somebody's made of it."	Inspector Goole	Act One
"Did it make much difference to her?"	Sheila	Act Two
"No, not entirely... But you're partly to blame."	Inspector Goole	Act Two
"How could I know what would happen afterwards?"	Sheila	Act Two
"You see, we have to share something. If there's nothing else, we'll have to share our guilt."	Inspector Goole	Act Two
"You mustn't try to build up any kind of wall between us and that girl."	Sheila	Act Two
"No, he's giving us the rope – so that we'll hang ourselves."	Sheila	Act Two
"I've done nothing wrong – and you know it."	Mrs Birling	Act Two

"Mother, I think it was cruel and vile."	Sheila	Act Two
"I blame the young man... He should be made an example of."	Mrs Birling	Act Two
"So he's the chief culprit anyhow."	Inspector Goole	Act Two
"You'll be able to divide the responsibility between you when I've gone."	Inspector Goole	Act Three
"This girl killed herself – and died a horrible death. But each of you helped to kill her. Remember that. Never forget it."	Inspector Goole	Act Three
"You can't do her any more harm. And you can't do her any good now, either. You can't even say 'I'm sorry Eva Smith.'"	Inspector Goole	Act Three
"We don't live alone. We are members of one body. We are responsible for each other."	Inspector Goole	Act Three
"You're the one I blame for this."	Mr Birling	Act Three
"Haven't I already said there'll be a public scandal – unless we're lucky – and who here will suffer from that more than I will?"	Mr Birling	Act Three
"The point is, you don't seem to have learnt anything."	Sheila	Act Three
"The money's not the important thing. It's what happened to the girl and what we all did to her that matters."	Eric	Act Three
"You're just beginning to pretend all over again."	Sheila	Act Three
"I don't see much nonsense about it when a girl goes and kills herself. You may be letting yourselves out nicely, but I can't."	Eric	Act Three
"But the whole thing's different now."	Mr Birling	Act Three
"Everything's all right now, Sheila."	Gerald	Act Three
"*As they stare guiltily and dumbfounded, the curtain falls.*"	Stage directions	Act Three

Loss of innocence

Quote	Character	Act
"I'm sorry, Daddy"	Sheila	Act One
"And if I could help her now, I would"	Sheila	Act One
"A nice little promising life there, I thought, and a nasty mess somebody's made of it."	Inspector Goole	Act One
"Why – you fool – he knows [...] And I hate to think how much he knows that we don't know yet. You'll see."	Sheila	Act One
"Don't interfere, please, Father."	Sheila	Act Two
"And you think young women ought to be protected against unpleasant and disturbing things?"	Inspector Goole	Act Two
"A pretty, lively sort of girl who never did anybody no harm."	Inspector Goole	Act Two
"What's the matter with that child?"	Mr Birling	Act Two
"She looked young and fresh and charming and altogether out of place down there."	Gerald	Act Two
"Your daughter isn't living on the moon. She's here in Brumley too."	Inspector Goole	Act Two
"You and I aren't the same people who sat down to dinner here."	Sheila	Act Two
"Silly boy!"	Mrs Birling	Act Two
"my child – your own grandchild – you killed them both – damn you, damn you"	Eric	Act Three
"If you want to know, it's you two who are being childish – trying not to face the facts."	Sheila	Act Three
"It's all right saying that now."	Sheila	Act Three
"I do take some interest in it. I take too much, that's my trouble."	Eric	Act Three
"And it frightens me the way you talk, and I can't listen to any more of it."	Sheila	Act Three

Duty and truth

Quote	Character	Act
"No, thank you, Mr Birling. I'm on duty."	Inspector Goole	Act One
"It's my duty to ask questions."	Inspector Goole	Act One
"Well it's my duty to keep labour costs down"	Mrs Birling	Act One
"That's something I have to find out."	Inspector Goole	Act One
"I'm trying to tell the truth. I expect you've done thighs you're ashamed of too."	Sheila	Act One
"Why – you fool – *he knows*. Of course he knows. And I hate to think how much he knows that we don't know yet. You'll see. You'll see."	Sheila	Act One
"Apologize for what – doing my duty?"	Inspector Goole	Act Two
"Public men, Mr Birling, have responsibilities as well as privileges."	Inspector Goole	Act Two
"I consider I did my duty." / "I consider it your duty."	Mrs Birling	Act Two
"That's what I meant when I talked about building up a wall that's sure to be knocked flat. It makes it all the harder to bear."	Sheila	Act Two
"[*rather wildly, with laugh*]: No he's giving us rope – so that we'll hang ourselves."	Sheila	Act Two
"You gave yourself away at once."	Inspector Goole	Act Two
"You told her. Why, you little sneak!"	Eric	Act Three
"I understand a lot of things now I didn't understand before."	Mr Birling	Act Three
"I've got to cover this up as soon as I can."	Mr Birling	Act Three
"trying not to face the facts"	Sheila	Act Three

"That's what's important – and not whether a man is a police inspector or not."	Sheila	Act Three
"Was it a hoax?"	Gerald	Act Three
"I don't see much nonsense about it when a girl goes and kills herself."	Eric	Act Three
"The whole damned thing can have been a piece of bluff!"	Mr Birling	Act Three
"No police enquiry. No one girl that all this happens to. No scandal"	Mr Birling	Act Three
"Proof positive! The whole story's just been a lot of moonshine."	Mr Birling	Act Three
"If it didn't end tragically, then that's lucky for us."	Sheila	Act Three
"whoever that Inspector was, it was anything but a joke... You began to learn something. And now you've stopped."	Sheila	Act Three

Section 8

Sample Essays

Essay 1

QUESTION: How does Priestley present Inspector Goole in *An Inspector Calls*? Write about:

- how the Inspector treats and deals with the other characters
- how Priestley presents the Inspector by the ways he writes

ESSAY	COMMENTS
INTRODUCTION In *An Inspector Calls*, J. B. Priestley presents Inspector Goole as[1] a commanding and morally authoritative[2] figure whose presence in the Birling household exposes the social injustices of early 20th century Britain. Through his deliberate speech, rhetorical control, and strategic interrogation,[2] the Inspector acts as Priestley's dramatic mouthpiece, advocating for collective responsibility in a world fractured by class divides. As the dramatic catalyst of the play,[3] Goole is portrayed not only as a lawful investigator but also as an agent of social conscience. Priestley uses him to subvert the traditional Edwardian power structures and to argue that moral accountability transcends class.[4]	1. Clearly establishes the central contention in the first sentence, directly addressing the essay question. 2. Characterises the Inspector's function using evaluative language ("commanding," "morally authoritative"). 3. Uses literary metalanguage (e.g. "dramatic mouthpiece", "catalyst") to indicate we are analysing the text, not summarising it! 4. This frames the Inspector ideologically as a representation of Priestley's socialist values.

PARAGRAPH 1	
Priestley presents Inspector Goole as a dominant and authoritative force to challenge the traditional class hierarchy.[5] From the moment of his arrival, the Inspector exerts control over the Birling household, disrupting its complacent, self-assured atmosphere. Priestley's stage direction that he speaks "weightily" suggests a deliberate gravitas in his tone,[6] implying that his words carry significant moral weight. The adverb[7] signals to the audience that Goole is a figure not to be dismissed – he demands attention and respect. His dominance is also made clear through stage directions such as "[massively taking charge]", where the adjective "massively" conveys both physical and rhetorical authority. The Inspector's interrogative style, marked by blunt, clipped questions like "Why?" and "As what then?" cuts through the Birlings' evasions and self-justifications.[8] This stark, minimalist syntax contrasts sharply with the affluent verbosity of characters like Mr Birling, reinforcing Goole's role as a truth-seeker. Most significantly, he delivers Priestley's core ideological message: "We are members of one body. We are responsible for each other." The body metaphor functions as a symbol of interconnectedness, suggesting that society must function collectively rather than in fragmented, self-interested units.[9] Priestley uses the Inspector's moral dominance to critique Edwardian class privilege and to reposition working-class suffering as a shared social failing.[10]	5. This paragraph opens with a clear topic sentence linking to the essay question. 6. Embeds quotations from stage directions (e.g. "weightily") and explains their effect. 7. Uses metalanguage to demonstrate textual awareness. Even if you can't find a specific literary device to analyse, you can comment on parts of speech like nouns, adjectives, adverbs, etc. or simply focus on the author's choice of words. 8. Analyses contrast between the Inspector's blunt style and the Birlings' verbosity. Even though this prompt focuses on the Inspector, there are lots of good opportunities to compare and contrast characters to make our points! 9. Connects textual analysis to broader themes of class and social order. 10. Concludes the paragraph by linking Goole's dominance to the play's social critique.

PARAGRAPH 2	
Priestley further uses the Inspector's rhetorical skill to expose hypocrisy and critique social injustice.[11] Inspector Goole's rhetorical power lies in his ability to hold a mirror to the Birlings' self-righteousness, often through dialogismus – quoting others to expose their contradictions.[12] When Mrs Birling dismisses Eva as a manipulative girl with "elaborate fine feelings and scruples that were simply absurd," the Inspector chillingly replies, "Her position now is that she lies with a burnt-out inside on a slab." The repetition of her language followed by brutal imagery confronts the audience with the real-life consequences of the family's actions. This emotional juxtaposition forces both character and audience to reckon with their complicity. Furthermore, Goole's approach shifts depending on the character he interrogates.[13] He is gentler with Sheila, acknowledging her potential for moral growth, and encourages Gerald to be honest with her: "She'll be alone with her responsibility, the rest of tonight, all tomorrow, all the next night." The anaphora[14] of "all" extends the sense of emotional burden, suggesting that accountability is personal and enduring.[15] By contrast, his terse reply to Gerald "[harshly] Yes, she's dead" marks a deliberate emotional distancing. The Inspector's shifting tone reinforces Priestley's critique of those who fail to evolve ethically. Through these interactions, Goole becomes the embodiment of justice, dividing characters by their willingness to accept responsibility.	11. Strong topic sentence outlining the rhetorical function of the Inspector. 12. Identifies dialogismus and explains its purpose effectively. 13. Highlights contrasting treatment of Sheila and Gerald to reveal the Inspector's moral compass. 14. Identifies literary techniques whilst maintaining a clear and coherent focus on the text's meaning in response to the prompt. 15. Embeds Priestley's critique of generational differences and emotional accountability.

PARAGRAPH 3 Through the Inspector, Priestley advocates for social change and critiques capitalist ideology. Priestley imbues the Inspector with an explicitly political role, positioning him as a moral counterweight to capitalist figures like Mr Birling.[16] Early in the play, Birling proclaims that "a man has to mind his own business and look after himself and his own," a philosophy the Inspector dismantles by unveiling the consequences of such selfishness. The Inspector's presence, timing, and symbolism all align with a Socialist worldview. His sudden arrival with the "sharp ring of a front door bell" interrupts Birling's speech, symbolising a rupture in the complacent status quo. The word "sharp" denotes urgency and disrupts the bourgeois setting.[17] Moreover, Goole's final speech includes prophetic warnings: "If men will not learn that lesson, then they will be taught it in fire and blood and anguish." This triplet, reminiscent of the apocalyptic tone of wartime rhetoric,[18] evokes the violence of both World Wars and reminds Priestley's 1945 audience of the real-world cost of social neglect. Historically, Priestley, himself a veteran of WWI and a supporter of the Labour Party, uses the Inspector to argue for a post-war world built on empathy and collectivism.[19] By the end of the play, Goole's role transcends that of a mere inspector; he becomes a symbolic force of social reckoning, demanding ethical introspection from both characters and audience.[20]	16. Compares Goole's ideas with Mr Birling's capitalist philosophy to highlight contrast. 17. Identifies the Inspector as symbolic as well as functional, linking this to the historical context of 1945 and Priestley's socialism. 18. Close analysis of "fire and blood and anguish" as a triplet and biblical allusion, linking the Inspector's speeches to wartime imagery to warn the audience. 19. Expands discussion beyond the play to its post-war reception. 20. Presents Goole as a moral and political disruptor, concluding by framing him as a symbol of "social reckoning."

CONCLUSION Through the character of Inspector Goole, Priestley constructs a dramatic figure who confronts privilege, unmasks hypocrisy, and voices the playwright's call for a more just and empathetic society. Goole's authority, rhetorical skill, and ideological purpose mark him as a vehicle for Socialist ideals, offering a powerful counter to Edwardian complacency. As a didactic figure, the Inspector forces the audience to question their own moral responsibilities in a fractured society. In doing so, Priestley not only critiques the past but also lays out a vision for a more unified, socially responsible future.[21]	21. A good conclusion does more than summarise – it amplifies your argument by bringing together your insights and linking them back to authorial intent and audience effect. Aim to leave the reader with a sense that you've uncovered not just what the character does, but why it matters socially, morally, and historically.

Essay 2

QUESTION: How does Priestley present what life is like for women in *An Inspector Calls*? Write about:

- what life is shown to be like for women in the play
- how Priestley presents what life is like for women

ESSAY	COMMENTS
INTRODUCTION In *An Inspector Calls,* J. B. Priestley critiques the patriarchal structure of Edwardian society by presenting women as constrained by gendered expectations and denied agency across social classes. Set in 1912 but written in 1945,[1] the play highlights how both working-class and upper-class women[2] suffer under male dominance, whether through condescension, abuse, or social rejection. Priestley uses his female characters to explore how misogynistic attitudes are upheld not only by men but also by women complicit in their own oppression.[3] This essay argues that Priestley presents women as victims of a rigid, patriarchal system in order to expose gender inequality and prompt his audience, particularly the post-war generation, to envision a more equitable society.	1. These opening sentences immediately identify the title, author, context, and link to the question. Integrating both the 1912 setting and the 1945 context is a great way to add sophistication to your essays. 2. Frames the issue around both class and gender. 3. This shows understanding of Priestley's authorial intent, linking his message about gender equality to the decisions he makes in the text in terms of characterisation and plot.

PARAGRAPH 1 Through the character of Sheila Birling, Priestley critiques the infantilisation and emotional suppression of upper-class women in Edwardian society.[4] At the start of the play, Sheila's engagement is celebrated not for love, but for its social utility. Despite being old enough to marry, she is still called a "child" by her mother, suggesting that she is viewed as immature and incapable of independent thought.[5] This infantilising metaphor reinforces the notion that women were denied full participation in adult life. Gerald's attempt to shield Sheila from the truth further reveals these patronising attitudes, prompting the Inspector's rhetorical challenge: "And you think young women ought to be protected against unpleasant and disturbing things?" Priestley's repetition of Gerald's sentiment emphasises the absurdity of shielding women from reality, highlighting the restrictive control exercised over them. Sheila's evolving emotional maturity and growing moral awareness throughout the play position her as a character who learns from her mistakes, yet her attempts to engage seriously are met with dismissal. When Sheila expresses concern, her mother labels her "hysterical," a term loaded with historical connotations of female irrationality.[6] By invoking this term, Priestley draws attention to the medicalised and gendered dismissal of women's emotions. Through Sheila, Priestley critiques the generational transmission of sexist norms and the social structures that silence women's voices and curtail their autonomy.[7]	4. Opens with a clear topic sentence tied to essay question. 5. Even one-word quotes can lead to valuable analysis. It's always better to be precise and include shorter quotes than to insert long lines of dialogue straight from the play (as the marker won't know that you understand which language is actually important in constructing meaning!). 6. Analyses "hysterical" as a gendered label, connecting the language to the social attitudes embedded within it, and balancing relevant contextual information with a focus on textual analysis. 7. Ends with a sentence linking Priestley's construction of this theme to his broader generational critique.

PARAGRAPH 2

Priestley also uses Mrs Birling to expose how women can become enforcers of the very patriarchal standards that oppress them. Described in the opening stage directions as a "rather cold woman," Mrs Birling embodies emotional detachment and moral superiority, traits associated with the Victorian ideal of female decorum. Her dismissal of Sheila's concerns and her own past acceptance of marital neglect evident in lines like "you'll have to get used to that, just as I did" reflects her resignation to a system in which women are expected to tolerate emotional abandonment.[8] Priestley uses Mrs Birling's role in the charity to illustrate her internalised class and gender prejudice. She labels Eva Smith's appeal for help as "gross impertinence," suggesting that she saw Eva's assertiveness as inappropriate for a woman of her class.[9] Mrs Birling's exclamation of "as if a girl of that sort would ever refuse money!" reveals her deep-seated contempt for working-class women, equating poverty with moral corruption. The forceful punctuation amplifies her scorn. Through this character, Priestley critiques the social divisions that pit women against one another and shows how even those who might advocate for other women can uphold systems of exclusion and judgement. Mrs Birling represents a generation resistant to change, reinforcing Priestley's argument that social reform must come from those willing to challenge inherited prejudices.

8. This is a clear point of contrast between Mrs Birling and Sheila – where one seems to be ready to forever tolerate her husband's dominance, the latter is willing to walk away from an engagement when she is dissatisfied with his behaviour. You can use contrasts like this between characters to sharpen your argument. Focus on how dialogue and diction expose deeper social flaws.
9. This analysis of class bias demonstrates how Mrs Birling upholds patriarchal social norms, thereby emphasising the way gendered conflict impacts women.

PARAGRAPH 3	
Eva Smith serves as the clearest representation of the powerlessness experienced by women under intersecting systems of class and gender. Her absence from the stage is a deliberate structural decision, symbolising the erasure of working-class women's voices from public and private discourse.[10] Each character's interaction with her contributes to her downfall, but perhaps most telling is Eric's admission: "I was in that state when a chap easily turns nasty." This vague and euphemistic phrasing masks the implication of coercion or even sexual violence, reflecting the casual misogyny embedded in male privilege.[11] The Inspector's condemnation of Eric, highlighting how he treated Eva "as if she were an animal," dehumanises Eric's actions while calling attention to the broader societal objectification of women. The animal metaphor[12] underscores Eva's reduction to a mere vessel for male desire, deprived of agency or dignity. Priestley uses Eva's narrative to indict the systemic exploitation of vulnerable women and to provoke guilt and reflection in both the characters and the audience. Her story, though silent, becomes the moral centre of the play, illustrating how patriarchal and capitalist forces combine to strip women of identity and humanity.	10. Establishes Eva's absence as symbolic, and frames her as the play's moral centre. Remember that you can use absences and silences in the play as part of your argument. 11. Quotes Eric's line to explore euphemistic violence. Note that we don't just let the quote speak for itself – we're using specific vocabulary to explain its meaning and effect. 12. Interprets "animal" metaphor as dehumanising, integrating commentary on the intersection of class and gender to add more depth while still staying within the confines of the essay question.

CONCLUSION	
Through his portrayal of Sheila, Mrs Birling, and Eva Smith, Priestley crafts a powerful critique of Edwardian gender inequality, emphasising that patriarchal oppression affects women across class lines. Whether infantilised, dismissed, or silenced, the female characters in *An Inspector Calls* reveal the damaging effects of societal norms that restrict women's autonomy and moral authority. Priestley warns that unless these attitudes are recognised and reformed, history will continue to repeat itself. By encouraging post-war audiences to reflect on their own values, he champions a future where gender equality and social justice are central to collective responsibility.	13. This conclusion does its job by reiterating core argument without repeating phrasing from the introduction, and using evaluative/analytical words like "damaging," "warns," and "champions" to comment on Priestley's moral and political intent.

Essay 3

QUESTION: How does Priestley explore responsibility in *An Inspector Calls*? Write about:

- the ideas about responsibility in *An Inspector Calls*
- how Priestley presents these ideas by the ways he writes

ESSAY	COMMENTS
INTRODUCTION J. B. Priestley's *An Inspector Calls* presents a powerful critique[1] of social inequality in Edwardian Britain, using the play to explore the conflict between individualism and collective responsibility. Written in 1945 and set in 1912, Priestley's play uses dramatic irony, characterisation, and the figure of Inspector Goole to encourage his post-war audience to reconsider how individuals and society should treat the vulnerable. Throughout the text, Priestley promotes the necessity of collective social responsibility through the downfall of the Birling family and the moral awakening of characters like Sheila, ultimately urging the audience to reflect on their own role within a wider community.[3]	1. Establishes the formal tone and clear focus of the essay. 2. Contextualises the play by referencing its pre-war setting and post-war production. 3. This shows awareness of authorial intent and Priestley's social agenda while laying out the direction of our argument, naming Sheila and the Inspector as key vehicles through which Priestley explores these themes.

PARAGRAPH 1 Priestley initially explores the dangers of individual responsibility through the character of Mr Birling, whose capitalist values and social conservatism embody Edwardian privilege.[4] Mr Birling's dismissal of collective thinking is evident when he declares that it is "nonsense" to believe people should act "like bees in a hive." The simile, drawing on the image of cooperative insects, symbolises a socialist ideal of unity and shared labour.[5] Mr Birling's derogatory tone and choice of the word "nonsense," which connotes absurdity, reveals his contempt for such ideas. Through this, Priestley positions Mr Birling as a mouthpiece for individualism and self-interest. His further remark that "a man has to mind his own business and look after himself and his own" reflects his refusal to acknowledge wider social obligations. However, his earlier claims – such as the assertion that war is impossible – are undermined through dramatic irony,[6] exposing him as ignorant and unreliable. By presenting Mr Birling as both morally and intellectually flawed, Priestley critiques those who ignore their social responsibilities in favour of personal gain.[7]	4. The topic sentence directly links Mr Birling to the essay question and identifies him as a symbol of Edwardian individualism and capitalism. 5. Effectively analyses the "bees in a hive" simile, linking it to socialism and Priestley's views and values. 6. Incorporates analysis of dramatic irony to show how Priestley undermines Birling, connecting characterisation to authorial intent and Priestley's critique of the elite. 7. Ends with a clear concluding sentence linking analysis back to responsibility

PARAGRAPH 2 In contrast to her father,[8] Priestley uses Sheila Birling to represent moral growth and an embrace of collective responsibility. While initially complicit in Eva Smith's downfall, Sheila's transformation becomes clear as she internalises the Inspector's message and begins to question her own privilege.[9] Her plea of "you mustn't try to build up a kind of wall between us and that girl" employs metaphor to condemn the class divisions separating rich and poor. The "wall" symbolises both social hierarchy and emotional detachment, suggesting that shielding oneself from the suffering of others is morally wrong.[10] Sheila's increasing use of imperative verbs like "mustn't" signals her shift from passive daughter to vocal moral agent. Priestley uses her to show that individuals can change when confronted with the truth, offering a hopeful contrast to her parents' stubbornness.[11] Her rejection of her parents' values illustrates the younger generation's openness to social progress, aligning with Priestley's belief in the potential for change after the trauma of war.[12]	8. Begins with a contrasting topic sentence to clearly differentiate Sheila from Birling. 9. Tracks Sheila's moral development across the play. 10. Focuses on a single, well-chosen quote and unpacks its metaphorical meaning. 11. Emphasises generational conflict, linking to social change. 12. Concludes by reaffirming Sheila as a model of collective responsibility.

PARAGRAPH 3	
The character of Inspector Goole functions as Priestley's moral voice, articulating the central message of collective responsibility.[13] Through him, Priestley delivers a direct challenge to individualism, especially when the Inspector describes Eva's story as a "chain of events." This metaphor evokes a sense of interconnection, where each "link" in the chain represents a moment of neglect by a different character.[14] It reflects the Socialist idea that actions have communal consequences. The Inspector's final speech[15] cements this ideology, warning that "if men will not learn that lesson, then they will be taught it in fire and blood and anguish." The tricolon of violent imagery in "fire and blood and anguish" alludes to the horrors of world wars, evoking a sense of apocalypse. This apocalyptic language serves as a warning to the audience, suggesting that failure to care for one another results in social collapse. By aligning the Inspector with moral authority and prophetic insight, Priestley urges the audience to recognise that social responsibility is not optional, but essential to avoid future tragedy.	13. States a clear topic sentence: the Inspector as the play's moral centre. 14. Analyses the "chain of events" metaphor in depth. 15. Use final speeches or monologues as key evidence – they often contain the writer's core message. In this case, the Inspector's speech shifts in tone from interrogative to prophetic, maintaining a consistent focus on collective responsibility and warning what could happen if society abandons such virtues.

CONCLUSION Through *An Inspector Calls*, Priestley makes a compelling case for collective responsibility, using the contrasting responses of his characters to Eva Smith's suffering to reflect broader ideological divides.[16] By exposing the dangers of selfishness through Mr Birling, celebrating personal transformation in Sheila, and articulating a moral warning through the Inspector, Priestley constructs a powerful argument for social reform. Ultimately, the play challenges audiences, then and now,[17] to reflect on their responsibility to others and to reject systems that allow suffering to go unnoticed.[18]	16. Restates the central contention clearly and confidently, synthesising the three body paragraphs without repeating. 17. This phrase allows us to comment on the past and present and how different audiences may respond differently due to their context and how social constructs evolve over time. 18. Ends on a high-impact note, reinforcing relevance and highlighting authorial intent.

Essay 4

QUESTION: How does Priestley use Eva Smith to represent poverty in *An Inspector Calls*?
Write about:

1. how Eva Smith is presented
2. how Priestley uses her to explore ideas about poverty and society

ESSAY	COMMENTS
INTRODUCTION In *An Inspector Calls*, J.B. Priestley presents poverty not simply as an economic condition but as a deeply moral and political concern, exposing its devastating effects on individuals through the character of Eva Smith.[1] Although she never appears on stage, Eva functions as a powerful dramatic device,[2] symbolising the exploited working class in Edwardian Britain. By constructing her story through the fragmented testimonies of the upper-class Birlings and Gerald Croft, Priestley critiques the systemic injustices of the time and challenges his post-war audience to reconsider their social responsibility. Hence, Priestley uses Eva Smith to foreground the vulnerability, dehumanisation, and moral dignity of the poor, ultimately advocating for greater social equality.[3]	1. Formal contention is clearly stated: Priestley uses Eva Smith to criticise poverty and class inequality. 2. Calling her a dramatic device highlights Eva's function as a constructed character by Priestley rather than pretending she is a real person, showing strong textual understanding. 3. This introduction has a good balanced focus, touching on structure, character function, and political message. It also directly engages with the essay question by using the 'impact of poverty' as the starting point for a discussion on themes of "vulnerability, dehumanisation, and dignity."

PARAGRAPH 1 Priestley presents Eva Smith as a symbolic representation of the working-class population, whose lives were often invisible and undervalued in early 20th century Britain. Her surname, "Smith," was one of the most common in the country, deliberately chosen to suggest that her suffering is not unique but representative.[4] This is confirmed by the Inspector's final speech, which references the "millions and millions of Eva Smiths and John Smiths left with us." The repetition of "millions" reinforces the scale of the problem, while the listing of "hopes and fears [...] sufferings [...] chance of happiness" humanises these nameless individuals, emphasising their emotional depth and dignity.[5] By aligning Eva with the masses, Priestley challenges his audience to see the working class not as a faceless entity but as real people deserving empathy. Furthermore, Eva's initial portrayal through Mr Birling, who describes her as a "good worker," reveals how the upper class reduces individuals to their economic utility. Mr Birling's lack of personal detail about her suggests a wilful indifference, symptomatic of a capitalist system that prioritises profit over people.[6] Through this symbolic construction, Priestley critiques how industrial capitalism dehumanises the working class, urging his audience to adopt a more compassionate, collective ethic.[7]	4. Name analysis: Explores "Smith" as a symbol – excellent close textual focus. 5. Quote analysis of "millions and millions. . . " is unpacked through repetition and listing. You don't always have to link a quote to a particular literary device, but it can be helpful to use this kind of metalanguage in order to explain its effect. 6. Here, we integrate historical insight to situate the treatment of workers in Edwardian industrial society, linking the ideas of individual suffering and collective suffering. 7. Strong concluding sentence: Returns to the idea of audience reflection and ethical reform.

PARAGRAPH 2	
Furthermore, Priestly explores the impact of poverty through Eva Smith's suffering, which unfolds as a gradual descent into destitution. Her transformation from an industrious employee to a woman "desperately hard up" reveals the fragility of working-class stability.[8] The adverb "desperately" conveys not only financial need but emotional despair, reflecting how economic hardship strips individuals of autonomy and dignity. The structure of the play in unveiling Eva's story backwards highlights the cumulative damage inflicted by repeated social failures. Each stage of her decline – job loss, homelessness, hunger, and unwanted pregnancy – exposes how poverty is not an isolated event but a relentless cycle. Yet, even in her suffering, Eva retains moral integrity.[9] She refuses to accept Eric's stolen money, insisting she "won't take any more," a decision that underscores her dignity despite her desperation. Through this, Priestley challenges the stereotype that poverty equates to moral weakness. Instead, he presents Eva as a morally upright figure, victimised not by her character but by a society that denies her support.[10] By foregrounding her resilience and ethical stance, Priestley encourages the audience[11] to reject prejudiced views of the poor and instead consider the systemic roots of suffering.	8. Topic sentence clearly addresses "impact of poverty" through Eva's decline, noting how Priestley constructs her downfall chronologically. 9. This introduces some nuance to the discussion by considering the moral contrasts – Eva is shown to be principled even when she is maltreated and desperate, whereas most of the other characters are not even when they are in a position of privilege. 10. Challenge to stereotype: Priestley reframes poverty as structural, not personal failure. Our argument is that the text shows poverty to be cyclical and inescapable within current systems. 11. Always pair descriptive analysis (what happens to Eva) with interpretative analysis (what Priestley wants us to think or feel about it).

PARAGRAPH 3 Eva Smith's interactions with the upper-class characters expose how poverty is perpetuated by social prejudice.[12] Mr Birling dismisses her demand for higher wages by warning of the working class "asking for the earth." This hyperbolic metaphor reduces her reasonable request to irrational greed, revealing Birling's inability to comprehend working-class struggles.[13] His fear of redistribution reflects the self-interest of the capitalist elite, who see any challenge to profit as a threat to social order. Similarly, Mrs Birling's refusal to assist Eva at her charity is laced with moral superiority. Referring to Eva as "a girl of that sort" implies a judgemental dismissal rooted in classist assumptions about respectability.[14] The phrase generalises and dehumanises, showing how poverty is viewed not as misfortune but as a moral failing. These moments of prejudice demonstrate how systemic inequality is upheld not only by economic structures, but by attitudes that devalue the poor. By exposing the callousness of the Birlings, Priestley implores his audience to reject such dismissiveness and recognise the need for empathy and structural change.[15]	12. Topic sentence directly connects class prejudice to Eva's suffering. 13. Quote unpacked well: "Asking for the earth" is interpreted as hyperbole and elitism. 14. Moral language: "moral superiority" and "judgemental dismissal" clearly convey social critique. 15. When writing about social prejudice, focus on both language and ideology – what does the character say, and what does it reveal about their worldview. Focus on attitude as well as action: Prejudice is not just what they do, but how they think.

CONCLUSION	
Through the character of Eva Smith, Priestley powerfully critiques the social structures and attitudes that sustain poverty in Edwardian Britain. Her symbolic role, moral strength, and mistreatment by others work collectively to expose the deep injustices faced by the working class. By giving a voice to the voiceless and framing her story as a collective moral failure, Priestley compels his audience to reflect on their own responsibilities within society. *An Inspector Calls* ultimately becomes a call to action, urging for compassion, systemic reform, and the creation of a fairer, more humane world.[16]	16. As always, our conclusion effectively reiterates the argument without needlessly repeating points. It also emphasises insights about the audience impact and Priestley's moral stance, which is should be a core consideration by the end of any essay.